The Ultimate Lebanese Cookbook

111 Dishes From Lebanon To Cook Right Now

Slavka Bodic

Imprint: Independently published

Please sign up for free Balkan and Mediterranean recipes:
www.balkanfood.org

Introduction

Do you want to enjoy and celebrate the authentic Lebanese flavors by cooking some delicious and savory meals at home? Then you have found a perfect read for you! This cookbook is about to introduce you to some of the most popular Lebanese recipes and meals that you'll definitely love, especially if you're an exotic food lover. Whether you've been to Lebanon or not, you can recreate its traditional cuisine at home with the help of this comprehensive cookbook. Lebanon is popular for its unique culture, languages and food and this book is one good way to come close to the flavorsome cuisine of this Middle Eastern state.

The Ultimate Lebanese Cookbook will introduce Lebanese cuisine and its culinary culture in a way that you may have never experienced before. It brings you a variety of Lebanese recipes in one place. The cookbook is great for all those who always wanted to cook Lebanese food on their own without the help of a native Lebanese. With this Lebanese cuisine cookbook, you can create a complete Lebanese menu of your own, or you can try all the special Lebanese recipes on different occasions as well. In this cookbook you'll find popular Lebanese meals and ones that you might not have heard of. From a variety of cakes to the luscious range of bread, warming soups, Lebanese desserts, drinks, and Lebanese salads, etc., you can uncover them all. And all these recipes are created in such a simple way that those who aren't even familiar with the Lebanese culture, food, and language can still try and cook them at home without facing much difficulty.

Lebanese culinary culture and cuisine are indeed full of wonders. There's a great use of sauerkraut, cabbage, beets, and cherries. And, if you want to add all those nutri-dense ingredients to your routine diet, then give this book a thorough read, and you'll discover all your answers right away.

What you can find in this cookbook:
- Insights about Lebanese Cuisine
- Facts About Lebanon
- Lebanese Breakfast Recipes
- Appetizers
- Soups
- Main Dishes and Salads
- Lebanese Desserts and Drinks

Let's try all these Lebanese Recipes and recreate a complete menu to celebrate the amazing Lebanese flavors and aromas.

Table of Contents

Why Lebanese Cuisine?

The most inspiring thing about Lebanese Cuisine is that it offers you a variety of healthy ingredients in such flavorsome combinations that you cannot even anticipate. Take the Fattoush salad, for example; a simple mix of garden vegetables turns to be super tasty and nutritious when served in Lebanese Style. The ingredients that we commonly find in Lebanese Cuisine include:

- Eggplant
- Chickpeas
- Lamb, chicken, and beef meat
- Lentils
- Olives
- Bharat and Za'atar spice
- Sugar syrup
- Pistachios
- Strained Yogurt

The Lebanese breakfast is the most tempting of all; it's perfect for giving you a kicking start for the day. With a wide range of vegetables, grains, legumes, and dairy; you can find them all in your Lebanese breakfast. On this menu, you can have a Lebanese egg Shakshuka or Labneh yogurt, all served with olive and delicious Hummus. In this way, you get to eat all the fiber-rich vegetables, protein-filled eggs, and dairy, along with the beans and peas.

When it comes to Lebanese sides, snacks or appetizers, and entrees, there are interesting options on the menu. You must have heard about most of these meals as today they're popular in various parts of the world:

- Hummus: a dip made from mashed chickpeas

- Labneh: strained yogurt
- Tabbouleh: bulgur salad with mint, parsley, tomato, and spring onion
- Mutabal: mashed eggplant with tahini, salt, olive oil, and garlic
- Moussaka: Grilled eggplant with tomato, olive oil, onion, and garlic
- Fattoush: Garden vegetable salad with toasted pita bread

Besides these popular meals from Lebanon, I personally enjoy Lebanese street food. The shawarma is a pure delight, as it offers you everything in a single bread wrap. Then there's Booza, which is a special ice-cream and a Lebanese specialty.

For dessert, the Lebanese Nights Dessert (Layali Lubnan) certainly has no parallel. And the Lebanese Osmalieh Vermicelli is the most irresistible sweet from this menu. Then sample both the Lebanese Bread Pudding and Lebanese Rice Pudding that you can enjoy in this cuisine as well.

Lebanon

L ebanon or the Lebanese Republic is a Levant region country present in Western Asia and the transcontinental region of the Middle East. To the north and east, it shares its border with Syria and to the south with Israel, while Cyprus is located on its west but across the Mediterranean Sea. It's mainly located at the crossroads of the Arabian hinterland and Mediterranean Basin and has remained part of the rich history of this region. However, it received a cultural, ethnic, and religious diversity of its own. With a 10,452 km2 land area, it's also one of the smallest recognized states on the Asian continent. Arabic is the official and most common language spoken in Lebanon.

From Christians to Arab Muslims, Maronites, Roman, and Druze, all at one point in history ruled and living in this land. And there's the reason that Lebanon is so culturally diverse. Beirut is one of the most visited cities in the region, and it's also known as the Paris of the Middle East. Geographically the country is divided into four distinct regions, the Lebanon mountain range, the coastal plain, the Anti-Lebanon Mountains, and the Beqaa valley. It has a moderate climate, and the coastal area is cool during winters and humid and hot during summers. The temperature goes below the freezing point in the mountainous regions.

People who have never been to Lebanon and have never explored many of its places and cities cannot fathom the beauty of its amazing landscapes and the ethnic diversity it received over the years. Most people get the idea of this land from the television content they watch, but Lebanon is much more than what you see on the screens. It has some amazing cities and diversely populated urban centers. Some of the best attractions in the country include:

- Kadisha Valley
- National Museum of Beirut
- Sursock Museum
- Temple of Bacchus
- Mzaar Ski Resort
- Hamra
- Cedars of God Bsharri
- Mohammed Alamin Mosque
- Baatara Waterfall
- Jbeil

My last visit to Lebanon had lent me several amazing sights and an unforgettable experience of getting to know the Lebanese food, the people, and the culture. The whole atmosphere captivates your mind and soul into it, and you feel like getting lost in the streets of this Middle Eastern beauty. If you too haven't been to Lebanon yet, then try its authentic meals and recipes from the cookbook and spread the traditional Lebanese aromas all around you.

Breakfast

Lebanese Street Bread (Kaak Alasreya)

Preparation time: 10 minutes
Cook time: 10 minutes
Nutrition facts (per serving): 216 Cal (14g fat, 4g protein, 1g fiber)

The famous Lebanese street bread is here to make your breakfast special. You can always serve this bread with a fresh berry smoothie.

Ingredients (6 servings)
2 lbs. 4 oz. all-purpose flour
½ teaspoon salt
⅓ cup sugar
2 cups lukewarm water
1 cup white sesame seeds
2 tablespoon instant yeast

Glaze
1 cup of water
2 tablespoon flour
2 tablespoon olive oil
A pinch of salt

Preparation
Mix the yeast with sugar and warm water in a bowl. Leave it for 5 minutes, add the flour and salt, and then mix well until smooth. Place this prepared dough in a greased bowl, cover, and leave for 1 hour. Divide the dough into 9 portions. Spread each dough portion on the working surface into ½ inch thick- 8 inch round circle. Use a 4 inch round cookie cutter to cut a hole at the center. Place the dough circles in a baking sheet lined with parchment paper. At 450 degrees F, preheat your oven. Prepare its glaze by mixing all its ingredients in a saucepan and cook until it thickens. Brush the glaze on

top of the dough rounds and drizzle sesame seeds on top. Bake them for 10 minutes in the preheated oven. Allow them to cool and then serve.

Lebanese Meat Pies (Sfeeha)

Preparation time: 15 minutes
Cook time: 12 minutes
Nutrition facts (per serving): 400 Cal (22g fat, 17g protein, 10g fiber)

You can give these meat-filled pies a try because they have a good and delicious combination of crispy dough stuffed with sautéed beef.

Ingredients (8 servings)
Dough
2 lbs. all-purpose flour
3 tablespoon sugar
2 tablespoon active dry yeast
1 tablespoon salt
¼ cup sunflower oil
2 ¼ cups whole milk

Meat filling
1 lb. 2 oz. minced lamb meat
2 small onions, diced
4 medium tomatoes, chopped
1 teaspoon salt
¼ teaspoon cinnamon powder, to taste
½ teaspoon seven spice powder
Chili flakes

Preparation
Mix the flour with the oil, salt, sugar, yeast, and milk in a bowl. Knead this dough for 3-5 minutes, then cover and leave for 1 hour. Meanwhile, blend the onions with the tomatoes in a blender until smooth. Transfer the tomatoes to a bowl and stir in the chili flakes, spices, salt, and minced meat.

Mix well and then strain the excess liquid. At 400 degrees F, preheat your oven. Divide the prepared dough into golf ball-sized balls and roll each ball into a ½ cm thick circle. Divide the beef filling at the center of each circle and pinch the two opposing edges of each circle to shape the sfeeha into a square boat. Place them in a greased baking sheet and bake for 12 minutes in the oven. Drizzle lemon juice on top. Serve.

Zaatar and Sumac Crackers

Preparation time: 15 minutes
Cook time: 20 minutes
Nutrition facts (per serving): 381 Cal (6g fat, 13g protein, 1g fiber)

If you're bored with the usual morning bread, then these Lebanese Zaatar crackers are one unique option to go for. Enjoy them with crispy bacon and eggs.

Ingredients (6 servings)
Dough
2 cups all-purpose flour
3 tablespoon olive oil
1 tablespoon sugar
⅔ cup warm water
½ teaspoon salt

Filling
½ cup zaatar
2 tablespoon sumac
⅓ cup sunflower oil
A pinch of sea salt

Preparation
At 300 degrees F, preheat your oven. Mix the flour with oil, salt, and sugar. Stir in warm water, mix well, and knead the dough until smooth. Divide this dough into three equal portions. Mix the sumac, zaatar, oil, and sea salt in a bowl. Roll each dough piece into 2 inches squares. Spread the zaatar filling on top and place them in a baking sheet lined with parchment paper. Bake for 20 minutes until golden brown. Serve.

Lebanese Cheese (Jibneh Baladi)

Preparation time: 5 minutes
Cook time: 10 minutes
Nutrition facts (per serving): 206 Cal (15g fat, 21g protein, 1g fiber)

Try the Lebanese cheese in the morning and make your breakfast super nutritious. Serve this cheese with a variety of bread and morning puddings.

Ingredients (6 servings)
4 ¼ quarts water
24 tablespoon full cream milk powder
½ cup white vinegar
4 teaspoon salt

Preparation
Mix water and milk powder in a saucepan and heat the mixture to 122 degrees F. Stir in the white vinegar and mix until it forms a curd. Leave it for 30 minutes. Strain this mixture through a cheesecloth, tie the cloth, and leave for 10 minutes in a colander. Transfer the strained mixture to a saucepan and add salt. Boil this mixture and mix well until smooth. Serve.

Flat Bread

Preparation time: 15 minutes
Cook time: 7 minutes
Nutrition facts (per serving): 204 Cal (4g fat, 5g protein, 1.4g fiber)

Try this Lebanese bread for breakfast, and you will forget about the rest. The recipe is simple and gives you soft and fluffy flatbreads that you can enjoy in a number of ways.

Ingredients (8 servings)
1 ¼ cup water
2 tablespoons olive oil
½ teaspoon white sugar
1 ½ teaspoon salt
3 cups flour
1 ½ teaspoon dry active yeast

Preparation
Add the yeast, sugar, and water to a mixing bowl, mix well, and then leave for 10 minutes. Stir in the oil, salt, and flour and then mix well until it comes together as smooth dough. Knead this prepared dough on a lightly floured surface and divide it into 8 equal parts. Spread each dough into a ⅛-inch-thick circle. Place the flatbread in baking sheets and bake them for 5-7 minutes in the oven at 475 degrees F, until golden brown. Serve warm.

Lebanese Traditional Breakfast

Preparation time: 10 minutes
Cook time: 10 minutes
Nutrition facts (per serving): 316 Cal (7g fat, 22g protein, 18g fiber)

Enjoy this fava bean meal on your Lebanese breakfast menu. Serve these beans with warm flatbread and yogurt.

Ingredients (6 servings)
3 (14 oz.) canned cooked fava beans
1 (15 ½ oz.) chickpeas canned
5 garlic cloves
1 lemon juiced
2 tablespoon tahini paste
1 teaspoon ground cumin
1 teaspoon salt
½ bunch parsley
1 tomato
Olive oil for serving

Preparation
Add fava beans and chickpeas to a cooking pot and heat for 10 minutes. Mix and ½ of this chickpea mixture with the crushed garlic, salt, lemon juice, tahini paste, and cumin. Add this mixture to the rest of the fava beans mixture and mix well. Stir in the tomatoes, parsley, and cayenne pepper. Drizzle olive oil on top and serve.

Meshtah

Preparation time: 10 minutes
Cook time: 15 minutes
Nutrition facts (per serving): 368 Cal (11g fat, 12g protein, 1g fiber)

Do you want to enjoy some pancake rolls with your favorite toppings on top? These apple cinnamon rolls are quick to make and easy to serve.

Ingredients (8 servings)
Dough
2 cups all-purpose flour
¼ cup canola oil
1 tablespoon active dry yeast
2 tablespoon fine bulgur
1 cup warm full cream milk
1 teaspoon salt
1 tablespoon sugar
1 ½ tablespoon anise seeds

Glaze
1 cup of water
2 tablespoon flour
2tablespoon olive oil
A pinch of salt
Topping
Sesame seeds

Preparation
Soak the bulgur in one cup of water for 30 minutes and then drain. Mix the flour with the yeast, bulgur, anise seed, salt, and sugar in a bowl. Stir in the oil and warm milk and then mix well until smooth. Cover and leave this dough for 2 hours. Prepare the glaze, mix all its ingredients in a saucepan,

and cook to a boil. Divide the prepared dough into 8 balls and roll each into 6 inches long and 1-inch thick bread. Place each bread on a baking sheet lined with parchment paper. Leave the bread for 8 minutes. At 400 degrees F, preheat your oven. Brush the glaze over the bread and drizzle sesame seeds on top. Bake the bread in the preheated oven for 10-15 minutes until the bread is golden brown. Slice and serve warm.

Lebanese Sweet Fritters (Zalabia)

Preparation time: 10 minutes
Cook time: 20 minutes
Nutrition facts (per serving): 244 Cal (10g fat, 8g protein, 2.5g fiber)

These sweet fritters are a classic Lebanese meal, great for breakfast and for side meals. You can try these fritters with cheese dip or a fruit smoothie.

Ingredients (6 servings)
2 ½ cups all-purpose flour
¼ cup canola oil
3 tablespoon sugar
2 tablespoon white sesame seeds
2 tablespoon whole anise seeds
1 tablespoon powdered milk
1 cup lukewarm water
1 ½ tablespoon active dry yeast
3 cups canola oil for deep frying

Preparation
Mix the anise seeds, sesame seeds, dry yeast, flour, sugar, milk, and oil in a bowl. Stir in the lukewarm water and then mix well. Knead this dough until smooth, cover and leave this dough for 1 hour. Divide the prepared dough into 22 balls. Roll each dough piece into ½ thickness. Cut three holes at the center and leave them for 25 minutes. Add the oil to a cooking pot and heat for deep frying. Deep fry the dough in the hot oil until golden brown. Place the fried fritters on a plate using a slotted spoon. Serve.

Bagels with Zaatar and Labneh

Preparation time: 15 minutes
Cook time: 22 minutes
Nutrition facts (per serving): 320 Cal (25g fat, 15g protein, 5.4g fiber)

It's about time to try some Lebanese bagels with zaatar and labneh on the breakfast menu and make it taste more diverse in flavors. Serve warm fresh from the oven.

Ingredients (8 servings)
3 ½ cups bread flour
1 ½ tablespoon sugar
2 teaspoon active dry yeast
1 ¼ cups lukewarm water
1 ½ teaspoon salt
1 ½ tablespoon honey, for the boiling water

Preparation
Mix flour with salt, dry yeast, and sugar in a large ceramic bowl. Stir in the lukewarm water and then mix well until smooth. Cover and leave this dough for 2 hours. Divide the dough into 8 equal-sized balls. Shape each piece into a bagel and place them on a baking sheet. Cover and refrigerate for 7 hours. At 425 degrees F, preheat your oven. Boil water in a cooking pot along with honey. Add 3 bagels to this mixture and cook for 1 minute per side. Transfer the bagels to a plate using a slotted spoon. Cook the remaining bagels in the same way. Place all the bagels on a baking sheet and drizzle zaatar on top and bake for 20 minutes until golden brown. Allow bagels to cool and serve.

Shakshuka

Preparation time: 15 minutes
Cook time: 29 minutes
Nutrition facts (per serving): 306 Cal (15g fat, 7g protein, 2g fiber)

The Lebanese shakshuka is a delicious morning meal you can try every day; it's best to serve with butter on top and toasted bread on the side.

Ingredients (4 servings)
2 tablespoon olive oil
1 onion, peeled and diced
3 garlic cloves, peeled and sliced
1 chili pepper, stemmed, sliced, and deseeded
1 ½ teaspoon salt
1 teaspoon black pepper
1 teaspoon paprika, smoked
1 teaspoon caraway seeds, crushed
1 teaspoon cumin seeds crushed
½ teaspoon turmeric
2 pounds ripe tomatoes, cored and diced
2 tablespoon tomato paste
2 teaspoon honey
1 teaspoon red wine vinegar
1 cup loosely packed greens, chopped
4 oz. feta cheese, cubed
4 eggs

Preparation
Sauté the onions and the garlic with oil in a skillet for 5 minutes. Stir in the spices, black pepper, salt and chili pepper and then sauté for 1 minute. Add the vinegar, honey, tomato paste, and tomatoes and then cook for 15 minutes with occasional stirring. Add the chopped greens and make six wells

in the mixture. Crack one egg into each well, cover, and cook for 8 minutes on low heat. Add the feta cheese to the mixture. Leave for 5 minutes and serve.

Fetteh

Preparation time: 15 minutes
Cook time: 20 minutes
Nutrition facts (per serving): 213 Cal (20g fat, 12g protein, 7g fiber)

The Lebanese chickpea fetteh breakfast is prepared with basic ingredients, yet it tastes so delicious. Serve it with warm buns and crispy bacon.

Ingredients (6 servings)
2 pounds of Greek yogurt
2 loaves of pita bread
16 oz. can of chickpeas
2 tablespoon tahini
½ of a lemon
6 garlic cloves
4 tablespoon olive oil
1 tablespoon salt
1 tablespoon black pepper
1 teaspoon of cumin
1 cup of pine nuts
¼ stick of butter
1 teaspoon of baking soda
Parsley, to garnish

Preparation
Cook the chickpeas with baking soda in a cooking pot to warm them up. Cut the pita bread into squares and sear in a skillet greased with cooking oil until golden brown. Mix the yogurt with the garlic, black pepper, salt, lemon juice, and tahini in a bowl. Sauté the pine nuts with butter in a skillet until golden brown. Place the pita bread on the serving plate and top it with the yogurt mixture and chickpeas. Garnish with cumin and parsley. Serve.

Batata Hara

Preparation time: 10 minutes
Cook time: 20 minutes
Nutrition facts (per serving): 321 Cal (10g fat, 12g protein, 2g fiber)

It's as if the Lebanese menu is incomplete without this potato batata harra breakfast. It's Lebanon's special inspired morning meal to serve.

Ingredients (6 servings)
6 potatoes, peeled and cubed
4 tablespoon olive oil
Olive oil
2 bunches of cilantro, chopped
1 white onion, chopped
4 jalapenos, chopped
10 garlic cloves, minced
Salt, to taste
Black pepper, to taste
Garlic powder, to taste

Preparation
Sauté the potatoes with the oil and salt in a skillet until golden brown. Sauté the onion, cilantro, jalapenos, and garlic in a skillet with 2 tablespoon oil until golden brown. Add the salt, garlic powder, and the remaining ingredients. Finally, mix well. Serve.

Za'atar Manaqis

Preparation time: 10 minutes
Cook time: 8 minutes
Nutrition facts (per serving): 243 Cal (11g fat, 15g protein, 1g fiber)

Best to serve at breakfast, this Zaatar Manaqis can function as a morning meal with eggs and crispy bacon. It's rich and loaded with calories and healthy fats.

Ingredients (4 servings)
Dough
1 cup lukewarm water
½ teaspoon sugar
2 ¼ teaspoon active dry yeast
3 cups unbleached all-purpose flour
1 teaspoon salt
2 tablespoon olive oil

Za'atar Topping
8 tablespoon Za'atar spice
½ cup Private Reserve olive oil

Serving
Fresh garden vegetables
Olives
Labneh or feta cheese

Preparation
Mix the water with yeast and sugar in a bowl and then leave for 10 minutes. Stir in the olive oil, salt, and flour and then mix evenly. Knead this dough for 10 minutes, cover, and leave for 30 minutes. Divide the dough into 8 balls. Place the balls in a baking sheet, cover and leave for 30 minutes. Mix

zaatar spices with olive oil in a bowl. At 400 degrees F, preheat your oven. Roll each dough ball into a 5-inch disc. Press the center of each disc and add 1 tablespoon Zaatar at the center. Place them in a baking sheet and then bake for 8 minutes at 400 degrees F. Allow the Manaqis to cool and serve.

Appetizers

Kibbe Balls

Preparation time: 15 minutes
Cook time: 30 minutes
Nutrition facts (per serving): 451 Cal (32g fat, 18g protein, 1g fiber)

The Lebanese kibbe balls are one of the most delicious street foods that you can try at home. It's known for its bulgur mixed beef taste and the energizing combination of ingredients.

Ingredients (6 servings)
1 cup fine bulgur, soaked
1 lb. ground beef
1 cup kamoune
2 cups hot water
2 teaspoon salt
1 teaspoon kibbeh spice mix

Filling
1 lb. ground beef
1 onion, chopped
3 tablespoon canola oil
¼ cup pine nuts
1 tablespoon seven spices
1 teaspoon salt
½ teaspoon black pepper

Kamoune
1 cup fine bulgur
½ onion, chopped
¼ cup red bell pepper, chopped
½ cup mint leaves, chopped
½ teaspoon dried marjoram

1 tablespoon kibbeh spice mix
1 teaspoon salt

Preparation

Soak the bulgur in hot water in a bowl for 30 minutes. Grind the kibbeh spices in a grinder. Prepare the kamouneh by blending all its ingredients into a food processor. For the filling, sauté the onion with 1 tablespoon Canola oil and pine nuts in a skillet until golden brown. Stir in the beef and sauté for 5 minutes until brown. Stir in the black pepper and the seven spices and then sauté for 3 minutes. For the kibbeh balls, soak the bulgur in water and drain. Mix the beef with the rest of the kibbeh spice, salt, and kammoune in a food processor. Take 2 tablespoon of the kibbeh dough and spread it into a round. Add a 1 tablespoon of filling at the center, wrap the dough around, and then roll into a ball. At 350 degrees F, preheat oil in a cooking pot. Deep fry the kibbeh balls until golden brown. Transfer the balls to a plate using a slotted spoon. Serve.

Muhammara

Preparation time: 10 minutes
Nutrition facts (per serving): 357 Cal (24g fat, 12g protein, 0g fiber)

Have you ever tried Lebanese Muhammara? Well, here's a recipe to make some with delicious roasted peppers and walnuts. Enjoy it with your favorite crackers or bread.

Ingredients (6 servings)
1 cup California walnuts, chopped
2 red peppers, chopped
2 garlic cloves, chopped
2 teaspoon red pepper paste
2 tablespoon pomegranate molasses
1 cup breadcrumbs
¼ cup olive oil
1 teaspoon Aleppo pepper, chopped
1 teaspoon salt
1 teaspoon cumin

Preparation
Blend the roasted red peppers with the red peppers and the rest of the ingredients in a blender. Serve.

Tomato and Onion Manakeesh

Preparation time: 10 minutes
Cook time: 12 minutes
Nutrition facts (per serving): 282 Cal (16g fat, 11g protein, 2g fiber)

Lebanese tomato and onion manakeesh make as excellent serving, which has the baked dough with tomato and onions mixture on top.

Ingredients (8 servings)
Dough
3 cups bread flour
1½ teaspoon active dry yeast
1 tablespoon white granulated sugar
1 cup warm water
⅓ cup olive oil
1 teaspoon salt

Topping
3 tomatoes, chopped
2 onions, chopped
1 tablespoon sumac
2 teaspoon salt
2 tablespoon olive oil

Preparation
Mix ½ cup warm water with sugar and yeast in a large bowl. Leave it for 10 minutes. Stir in the rest of the dough ingredients and then mix well. Knead this dough for 5 minutes. Cover and leave the dough for 1 hour. Divide the dough into 12 balls and leave them for 45 minutes. Drain the chopped onions and tomatoes. Roll out each dough ball into a 6 inch round. Place the rounds on a baking sheet. Mix the onions, oil, and tomatoes in a bowl

and divide over the dough. At 425 degrees F, preheat your oven. Bake the manakeesh for 12 minutes in the oven until golden brown. Serve.

Lebanese Beef Spring Rolls

Preparation time: 15 minutes
Cook time: 20 minutes
Nutrition facts (per serving): 299 Cal (8g fat, 28g protein, 1g fiber)

These beef stuffed beef spring rolls are here to complete your Lebanese snacks menu. These spring rolls are served as a side meal on all special occasions and celebrations.

Ingredients (8 servings)
10 sheets spring roll pastry
½ lb. ground beef
1 onion, chopped
2 tablespoon pine nuts
2 tablespoon olive oil
1 teaspoon 7 spices
1 teaspoon salt
¼ teaspoon black pepper
1 tablespoon flour
1 tablespoon water

Preparation
Sauté the pine nuts with tablespoon oil in a skillet until golden brown. Stir in the beef and then sauté until brown. Stir in the onion, black pepper, salt, and 7 spices and then sauté for 5 minutes. Mix the flour with water in a small bowl. Spread the roll wrappers on the working surface. Divide the beef filling at the center of each wrapper and wrap the wrapper into a roll. Seal the edges by dapping them with a flour paste. At 350 degrees, preheat the oil in a deep-frying pan. Add beef rolls and deep fry until golden brown. Transfer to a plate using a slotted spoon. Serve warm.

Olive Mini Pies

Preparation time: 15 minutes
Cook time: 25 minutes
Nutrition facts (per serving): 132 Cal (11g fat, 1.3g protein, 3g fiber)

These mini olive pies will satisfy your olive craving in no time. They're quick to make and bake if you have biscuit dough at home.

Ingredients (4 servings)
½-pound pitted green olives, chopped
2 red bell peppers
1 small onion, finely chopped
2 tablespoon olive oil
½ teaspoon sumac
Chili pepper, to taste
Ground black pepper, to taste
2 ready-made biscuit dough (10 counts each)

Preparation
At 375 degrees F, preheat your oven. Deseed the quartered peppers and rub them with olive oil. Spread the peppers on a baking sheet, bake for 15 minutes, and then allow them to cool. Chop the roasted peppers. Sauté the onion with olive oil in a cooking pan until soft. Stir in the chopped peppers and the remaining ingredients. Mix well. Place the biscuit dough on the baking sheet and divide the filling into each. Fold the edges of the dough of the biscuits around the filling and bake for 10 minutes. Serve warm.

Garlic Aioli (Toum)

Preparation time: 15 minutes
Nutrition facts (per serving): 296 Cal (6g fat, 23g protein, 2g fiber)

Garlic Aioli is a popular Lebanese side serving that is enjoyed all over the country. It has a delightful mix of garlic, lemon juice, and mayonnaise.

Ingredients (4 servings)
½ cup garlic cloves
1½ cup canola oil
2 tablespoon lemon juice
1 teaspoon salt
¼ cup mayonnaise

Preparation
Blend the garlic with 1 teaspoon salt and rest of the ingredients in a blender until smooth. Stir in ¼ cup mayonnaise and then mix well. Serve.

Hummus with Beef

Preparation time: 5 minutes
Cook time: 15 minutes
Nutrition facts (per serving): 356 Cal (22g fat, 17g protein, 0.3g fiber)

Lebanese hummus with beef makes a great serving if you're seeking a quick snack to make. Serve this hummus with delicious crackers and chips.

Ingredients (6 servings)
Hummus
2 cups chickpeas
2 tablespoon tahini paste
¼ cup lemon juice
2 small garlic cloves
2 tablespoon water
½ teaspoon salt
Olive oil for serving

Beef
½ lb. minced ribeye
2 tablespoon olive oil
½ teaspoon salt
1 teaspoon 7 spices
¼ teaspoon black pepper
3 tablespoon pine nuts

Preparation
Blend the chickpeas with tahini, lemon juice, garlic, water, and salt in a blender until smooth. Sauté the beef with oil, salt, 7 spices, black pepper, and pine nuts in a skillet until brown. Spread the hummus on the serving plate and top it with a drizzle of olive oil. Add the sautéed beef on top. Serve.

Sweet Pumpkin Hummus

Preparation time: 15 minutes
Cook time: 10 minutes
Nutrition facts (per serving): 354 Cal (35g fat, 5g protein, 1.4g fiber)

If you haven't tried the sweet pumpkin hummus before, then here comes a simple and easy to cook recipe that you can easily prepare and cook at home in no time with minimum efforts.

Ingredients (6 servings)
1 can (15.5 oz) of chickpeas
¾ cup pumpkin puree
1 tablespoon tahini paste
3 tablespoon maple syrup
1 tablespoon water
1½ teaspoon ground cinnamon
½ teaspoon salt

Pita chips
1 large pita bread
1 tablespoon olive oil
½ teaspoon salt
¼ teaspoon black pepper

Preparation
At 375 degrees F, preheat your oven. Layer a parchment paper with aluminum foil. Cut the pita bread into strips and toss with olive oil. Spread these strips in a baking sheet and drizzle black pepper and salt on top. Bake for 10 minutes until golden brown. Blend the chickpeas with the rest of the ingredients in a blender. Serve the hummus with pita chips on top.

Batata Soufflé

Preparation time: 15 minutes
Cook time: 60 minutes
Nutrition facts (per serving): 275 Cal (9g fat, 21g protein, 2g fiber)

This Lebanese batata souffle is loaded with potatoes and breadcrumbs, another Lebanese-inspired delight that you should definitely try on this cuisine.

Ingredients (6 servings)
7 russet potatoes, peeled and diced
6 tablespoon salted butter
½ cup whole milk
1 lb. ground beef
1 onion, chopped
2 tablespoon olive oil
1 tablespoon seven spices
4 teaspoon salt
1 teaspoon black pepper
½ cup Italian breadcrumbs

Preparation
Boil the potatoes with water and salt in a cooking pot for 20 minutes and then drain. Sauté the onion with oil, ½ teaspoon black pepper, 1 teaspoon salt, and 1 tablespoon seven spices in a skillet until soft. Stir in the beef and sauté until brown. At 375 degrees F, preheat your oven. Drain the boiled potatoes and mash them in a bowl. Stir in ½ cup milk, 4 tablespoon butter, ½ teaspoon black pepper, and 1 teaspoon salt, and then mix well. Mix the breadcrumbs with 2 tablespoon butter in a bowl. Grease a 12x7 inches baking dish with cooking spray. Spread half of the mashed potatoes in the casserole dish and top with the beef mixture. Add the remaining potato

mash and breadcrumbs on top. Bake for 30 minutes in the oven. Allow the soufflé to cool, slice, and serve.

Labneh Balls

Preparation time: 15 minutes
Nutrition facts (per serving): 245 Cal (10g fat, 13g protein, 2g fiber)

These simple, quick and easy labneh balls appetizer have no parallel. If you have some yogurt at home, then you can prepare it in no time.

Ingredients (6 servings)
2 (32oz.) containers yogurt
1 teaspoon salt
4 cups olive oil
2 tablespoon dried mint
2 tablespoon Aleppo pepper, chopped
2 tablespoon za'atar spice

Instructions
Layer a colander with cheesecloth. Add the yogurt to this cheese cloth and drizzle salt on top. Tie the cheesecloth and hand it over the bowl for 2 days. Once the yogurt is strained, make 50 balls from this mixture. Roll them in the zaatar spice and drizzle Aleppo pepper, mint, and oil on top. Serve.

Sfouf Mini Cakes

Preparation time: 10 minutes
Cook time: 22 minutes
Nutrition facts (per serving): 274 Cal (3g fat, 11g protein, 3g fiber)

Have you tried the famous sfouf mini cakes? If you haven't, now is the time to cook these delicious cakes at home using simple and healthy ingredients.

Ingredients (6 servings)
1½ cups all-purpose flour
½ cup fine semolina
1⅓ cup white granulated sugar
¾ cup water
¾ cup olive oil
1 tablespoon turmeric
1½ teaspoon baking powder
1 tablespoon raw slivered almonds

Preparation
Grease a 12-cup liner with a cooking spray. At 375 degrees F, preheat your oven. Mix the flour with the baking powder, turmeric, sugar, and semolina in a bowl. Stir in the water and the oil and then mix evenly. Divide this mixture into the muffin tray. Drizzle almonds on top and bake for 22 minutes in the oven. Allow the cakes to cool and serve.

Salads

Lebanese Fattoush Salad

Preparation time: 10 minutes
Cook time: 10 minutes
Nutrition facts (per serving): 261 Cal (3g fat, 15g protein, 1g fiber)

The Lebanese Fattoush salad has a rich combination of ingredients that you can easily prepare at home. The salad is fairly easy to make and doesn't require much cooking.

Ingredients (4 servings)
Salad
1 large double pita bread, cut into triangles
3 tablespoon olive oil
Salt, to taste
Black pepper, to taste
1 romaine lettuce head, chopped
1 large vine-ripe tomato, diced
3 Persian cucumbers quartered
½ green pepper chopped
5 radishes, diced
2 green onions, chopped
¼ cup parsley, chopped

Dressing
3 tablespoon olive oil
2 tablespoon lemon juice
2 garlic cloves, pressed
1 teaspoon lemon zest, grated
1 teaspoon pomegranate molasses
½ teaspoon mint fresh, grated
½ teaspoon salt
Black pepper, to taste

Preparation

Sauté the pita bread with 3 tablespoon olive oil in a skillet until golden brown. Season the pita bread with black pepper and salt. Mix the rest of the ingredients in a bowl. Mix the olive oil with the rest of the dressing ingredients in a bowl. Pour into the salad and then mix well. Garnish with pita bread and serve.

Lebanese Cucumber Salad

Preparation time: 15 minutes
Nutrition facts (per serving): 309 Cal (12g fat, 17g protein, 3g fiber)

Do you want to enjoy some cucumber on the menu with a Lebanese twist?
Then try this recipe and enjoy the best of all flavors in one single meal.

Ingredients (4 servings)
1 ½ cup parsley, chopped
5 tablespoon mint chopped
1 tablespoon bulgur
1 small cucumber, finely chopped
2 tablespoon warm water
2 tablespoon lemon juice
7 tablespoon olive oil
1 teaspoon salt
1 teaspoon black pepper
1 tomato, chopped
1 piece of lettuce, chopped

Preparation
Soak the bulgur in warm water in a bowl for 30 minutes and then drain. Mix
the rest of the ingredients in a salad bowl. Stir in the bulgur and mix well.
Serve.

Lebanese Roasted Vegetables with Lentils

Preparation time: 15 minutes
Cook time: 75 minutes
Nutrition facts (per serving): 277 Cal (24g fat, 10g protein, 3g fiber)

If you want some new and exotic flavors in your meals, then this Lebanese roasted vegetables with lentils recipe is best to bring that variety to the menu.

Ingredients (6 servings)
Spice mix
1 teaspoon sweet paprika
1 teaspoon cumin
1 teaspoon ground coriander
1 teaspoon cardamom
½ teaspoon cinnamon
½ teaspoon nutmeg

Salad
¾ cup uncooked beluga lentils
3 tablespoon olive oil
1 medium sweet potato, peel and cut in short wedges
1 sweet red pepper, sliced
2 carrots, peeled, and sliced
3 small red onion, cut into wedges
Salt and black pepper, to taste
fresh parsley, to garnish
½ cup walnuts, toasted

Yoghurt sauce
½ cup Greek yoghurt
4 tablespoon olive oil
Zest of ½ organic lemon

4 tablespoon lemon juice
1 tablespoon flat-leaf parsley, chopped

Preparation
At 400 degrees F, preheat your oven. Layer a baking sheet with parchment paper. Mix all the spice ingredients in a bowl. Cook the lentils, as per the package's instruction, in 3 times more water for 30 minutes and then drain. Toss the veggies with the spice mix, 2 tablespoon olive oil on a baking sheet, and bake for 30 minutes. Toss the veggies after 15 minutes. Mix all the yogurt sauce ingredients in a bowl. Add the lentils to the veggies and pour the sauce on top. Garnish with walnuts and parsley. Serve.

Tabbouleh

Preparation time: 10 minutes
Nutrition facts (per serving): 302 Cal (11g fat, 12g protein, 5g fiber)

The Lebanese Tabbouleh salad is enjoyed with all sorts of entrees, and it tastes great with sour cream on top. Have it at your dinner table for a tempting serving.

Ingredients (6 servings)
2 cups parsley, chopped
¼ cup fine bulgur
1 seeded tomato, diced
5 scallions, sliced
¼ cup mint, chopped
Juice of 2 lemons
4 tablespoon olive oil
½ teaspoon salt
Few grinds of black pepper
1 teaspoon crushed dried mint

Preparation
Soak the bulgur in cold water in a bowl for 15 minutes and then drain. Mix the bulgur with the rest of the ingredients in a salad bowl. Serve.

Lebanese Cucumber Tomato Salad with Mint

Preparation time: 5 minutes
Nutrition facts (per serving): 149 Cal (1g fat, 9g protein, 0.1g fiber)

This Lebanese Cucumber and Tomato salad is everyone's favorite go-to side meal. Full of calories and good taste, it's simple, easy to make, and doesn't involve all sorts of ingredients.

Ingredients (4 servings)
5-inch cucumbers, cut into chunks
3 beefsteak tomatoes, cut into chunks
1 sweet onion, sliced
2 garlic cloves, minced
15 leaves fresh mint, chopped
2 tablespoon crushed dried mint
4 tablespoon olive oil
Juice of 2 lemons
Salt and black pepper, to taste

Preparation
Mix the onion, tomatoes, and cucumbers with the rest of the ingredients in a salad bowl. Serve.

Radish Arugula Salad

Preparation time: 10 minutes
Nutrition facts (per serving): 51 Cal (4g fat, 1g protein, 1g fiber)

This Radish Arugula Salad has a delightful mix of arugula with radishes and onion. Serve this mix with all your entrees and a drizzle of pepper on top.

Ingredients (6 servings)
3 cups baby arugula
4 radishes, sliced
3 tablespoon onion, chopped
1 lemon
2 tablespoon olive oil
Salt, black pepper, to taste
Garlic powder, to taste

Preparation
Mix the radishes with the onion and the rest of the ingredients in a salad bowl. Serve.

Yogurt Cucumber Salad with Mint

Preparation time: 15 minutes
Nutrition facts (per serving): 144 Cal (17g fat, 16g protein, 1g fiber)

The refreshing cucumber salad is here to make your dinner menu a little more delicious and nourishing.

Ingredients (4 servings)
2 cups yogurt
1 garlic clove, minced
½ teaspoon salt
2 teaspoons crushed dried
2 tablespoon fresh mint, chopped
4 pickling cucumbers, sliced

Preparation
Mix the yogurt with the mint, salt, and garlic in a salad bowl and then stir in the rest of the ingredients. Mix well and serve.

Lebanese Potato Salad

Preparation time: 15 minutes
Cook time: 13 minutes
Nutrition facts (per serving): 183 Cal (4g fat, 5g protein, 0.1g fiber)

The appetizing and savory potato salad makes a great addition to the side menu, and it looks lovely when served at the table.

Ingredients (6 servings)
3 pounds russet potatoes, peeled and diced
2 teaspoon salt
Juice of three large lemons
¼ cup olive oil
1 cup scallions, sliced
¼ cup fresh mint, chopped

Preparation
Boil the potatoes in water with a teaspoon of salt in a saucepan for 13 minutes and then drain. Mix the potatoes with olive oil, lemon juice, and salt in a salad bowl. Stir in mint and scallions. Serve.

Grilled Corn Salad with Mint

Preparation time: 10 minutes
Cook time: 10 minutes
Nutrition facts (per serving): 223 Cal (5g fat, 14g protein, 1g fiber)

Here comes a fiber-rich mix of all native Lebanese ingredients, including grilled corn, mint, onion, and feta. Serve this salad with a drizzle of lemon juice on top.

Ingredients (6 servings)
8 cobs of corn, shucked
¼ cup olive oil
1 handful fresh mint, chopped
½ red onion, diced
½ cup crumbled feta
Juice of 1 lemon
1 pinch of salt
Black pepper, to taste

Preparation
Grill the corn cob on high heat from all the sides until lightly charred. Remove the kernels from the cob and transfer them to a salad bowl. Stir in the rest of the ingredients and then mix well. Serve.

Balela Salad

Preparation time: 10 minutes
Nutrition facts (per serving): 253 Cal (18g g fat, 29g protein, 3g fiber)

The famous Balela salad with beans is great to serve as a healthy side meal. Try making it at home with these healthy ingredients and enjoy it.

Ingredients (4 servings)
2 (15 oz.) cans garbanzo beans, rinsed and drained
1 (15 oz.) cans black beans, rinsed and drained
½ cup onion, chopped
1 jalapeno, chopped
½ cup sun-dried tomatoes
1 pint grape tomatoes, cut in half
⅓ cup fresh dill, chopped
⅓ cup fresh basil, chopped
⅓ cup fresh Italian parsley, chopped
¼ cup lemon juice
⅓ cup olive oil
2 garlic cloves, pressed
3 tablespoon apple cider vinegar
Salt and black pepper, to taste
Feta cheese, to taste

Preparation
Mix the beans with the onion and the rest of the ingredients in a bowl. Serve.

Chicken Shawarma Salad

Preparation time: 10 minutes
Cook time: 14 minutes
Nutrition facts (per serving): 243 Cal (13g fat, 4g protein, 0.2g fiber)

This colorful chicken shawarma salad is a Lebanese specialty, and it's served on all special occasions. It's prepared using a nice mix of avocado, olives, tomatoes, and lettuce.

Ingredients (4 servings)
Chicken Shawarma
2 tablespoon plain Greek yogurt
2 tablespoon olive oil
½ tablespoon tahini
2 garlic cloves, minced
¼ teaspoon ground cinnamon
¼ teaspoon ground coriander seed
¼ teaspoon ground cloves
¼ teaspoon ground cumin
¼ teaspoon ground fennel
¼ teaspoon smoked paprika
¼ teaspoon ground cardamom
¼ teaspoon cayenne pepper
½ teaspoon salt
4 boneless chicken thigh fillets

Salad
4 cup lettuce, shredded
2 tomatoes, diced
1 ripe avocado, diced
1 Lebanese cucumber, diced
½ red onion, chopped

½ cup Kalamata olives
⅓ cup crumbled feta
¼ cup fresh parsley, chopped

Garlic Yogurt Sauce
½ cup plain Greek yogurt
1 tablespoon tahini
1 garlic clove, minced
1 teaspoon lemon juice
Salt, to taste

Preparation
Mix all the ingredients for shawarma in a bowl, cover, and marinate for 2 hours. Grill the chicken in a greased grill pan for 7 minutes per side. Cut the seared bread into strips. Sauté the flatbreads with oil in a skillet until golden brown. Mix the rest of the ingredients in a salad bowl. Stir in the toasted bread and top with the grilled chicken. Serve.

Lebanese Lentil Salad with Garlic And Herbs

Preparation time: 10 minutes
Cook time: 30 minutes
Nutrition facts (per serving): 252 Cal (11g fat, 17g protein, 5g fiber)

The Lebanese lentil salad is one delicious way to complete your Lebanese menu; here's a recipe that you can try to have a delicious meal.

Ingredients (4 servings)
1 cup green lentils
4 tablespoon olive oil
12 garlic cloves, minced
¾ cup fresh mint, chopped
¾ cup fresh parsley, chopped
4 tablespoon lemon juice
1 ½ teaspoon ground cumin
¼ teaspoon ground allspice
Salt and black pepper, to taste

Preparation
Rinse and boil the lentils in a cooking pot with 3 cups water for 30 minutes and then drain. Mix the lentils with garlic, mint, parsley, lemon juice, cumin, allspice, black pepper, salt, and olive oil in a bowl. Serve.

Bean Salad

Preparation time: 10 minutes
Nutrition facts (per serving): 311 Cal (10g fat, 14g protein, 13g fiber)

A fava beans salad is the right fit to serve with your Middle Eastern entrees. Here the beans are mixed with chickpeas and veggies for a wholesome flavor.

Ingredients (4 servings)
1 cup small fava beans, cooked
1 cup chickpeas, cooked
2 medium tomatoes
½ cup chopped parsley
3 cloves mashed garlic
1 chopped green onion
3 tablespoons lemon juice
2 tablespoons olive oil
½ teaspoon cumin
Salt and black pepper, to taste

Preparation
Take a suitable salad bowl and add all the ingredients. Mix and toss well. Serve.

Lebanese Salad

Preparation time: 10 minutes
Nutrition facts (per serving): 280 Cal (5g fat, 12g protein, 2g fiber)

This Lebanese salad is made primarily from tomatoes, bell pepper, cucumber, green onion, and lettuce, which are then seasoned with zaatar and mint. The salad tastes great when served with sour cream and croutons.

Ingredients (4 servings)
3 medium tomatoes, diced
1 green bell pepper, seeded, chopped
½ of cucumber, seeded, chopped
5 green onions, chopped
¼ cup fresh parsley, chopped
1 small onion, chopped
Romaine lettuce, chopped

Dressing
¼ cup olive oil
¼ cup of lemon juice
2 garlic cloves, minced
1 teaspoon dried mint
1 teaspoon sumac or za'atar
½ teaspoon salt
Black pepper, to taste

Preparation
Prepare the dressing by mixing all its ingredients in a salad bowl. Stir in the rest of the ingredients and mix well. Serve.

Soups

Red Lentil Soup

Preparation time: 10 minutes
Cook time: 32 minutes
Nutrition facts (per serving): 327 Cal (15g fat, 10g protein, 1g fiber)

If you haven't tried the classic soup before, then here comes a simple and easy to cook recipe that you can recreate at home in no time with minimum efforts.

Ingredients (6 servings)
1 ½ cups red lentil
5 cups of water
½ cup carrots, chopped
1 celery stalk, chopped
1 medium onion, chopped
6 garlic cloves, chopped
½ tablespoon cumin powder
¼ teaspoon turmeric powder
½ teaspoon cayenne pepper
1 bay leaf
1 cube vegetable bouillon
Salt, to taste
½ tablespoon olive oil
Juice of ½ lemon
Parsley, chopped, for garnishing
Red chili flakes for garnishing

Preparation
Sauté the garlic, onion, and bay leaf with oil in a skillet until soft. Stir in the celery and carrot and then cook for 2 minutes. Stir in 1 teaspoon water, salt, vegetable bouillon, and the spices and then mix well. Add the lentils and water and then cook for 25 minutes. Discard the bay leaf from the soup and blend the rest with an immersion blender. Cook the soup for 5 minutes and then garnish with chili flakes, olive oil, lemon juice, and parsley. Serve warm.

Lebanese Lentil Soup with Greens

Preparation time: 15 minutes
Cook time: 55 minutes
Nutrition facts (per serving): 381cal (26g fat, 14g protein, 0.6g fiber)

The Lebanese lentil soup with greens has no parallel in taste. It has a mix of lentils and spinach. Enjoy this soup with crispy bread.

Ingredients (8 servings)
1 tablespoon olive oil
1 medium onion, diced
2 medium carrots, peeled and diced
3 stalks celery diced
4 garlic cloves, minced
2 teaspoon cumin
2 teaspoon cinnamon
1 cup brown lentils uncooked
4 cups chicken broth
4 cups of water
1 lemon juiced
Salt and black pepper, to taste
8 cups spinach

Preparation
Sauté the celery, carrots, and onions with oil in a skillet for 7 minutes. Stir in the black pepper, salt, cinnamon, cumin, and garlic and then sauté for 1 minute. Stir in the lentils, broth, lemon juice and water and then boil the mixture, reduce the heat, and cook for 45 minutes. Add the spinach and cook for 2 minutes. Stir in the lemon juice, black pepper, and salt. Serve warm.

Lebanese Vegetable Soup

Preparation time: 15 minutes
Cook time: 20 minutes
Nutrition facts (per serving): 248 Cal (8g fat, 12g protein, 1g fiber)

A perfect mix of veggies with chickpeas is all that you need to expand your Lebanese menu. Simple and easy to make, this recipe is a must to try.

Ingredients (4 servings)
1 Spanish onion, chopped
2 tablespoon olive oil
2 ½ cups carrots, chopped
¼ teaspoon ground red pepper
1 teaspoon ground coriander
4 garlic cloves, minced
1 ½ cups potatoes, chopped
1 teaspoon salt
4 cups vegetable stock
2 large tomatoes, chopped
10 artichoke hearts, cut into eighths
¾ cup canned chickpeas
¼ cup fresh parsley, chopped
2 lemons, cut into wedges

Preparation
Mix the vegetable stock, chickpea liquid, and artichoke heart brine in a bowl. Sauté the onion with olive oil for 5 minutes. Stir in the carrots, cover, and cook for 3 minutes. Add the garlic, coriander, and red pepper. Cover and cook for 3 minutes. Stir in the potatoes, 2 cups stock mixture and salt, cover, and cook the soup to a boil. Reduce the heat and cook the potatoes until soft. Stir in the chickpeas, artichoke hearts, and tomatoes. Adjust the

seasoning with salt, cover, and cook for 4 minutes. Garnish with lemon wedges and parsley. Serve warm.

Chicken Soup

Preparation time: 10 minutes
Cook time: 40 minutes
Nutrition facts (per serving): 368 Cal (21g fat, 8g protein, 1g fiber)

Serve the warming bowl of chicken soup and make your meal a little more nutritional. It has everything healthy in it, ranging from chicken to herbs, etc.

Ingredients (4 servings)
4 (2 lbs.) chicken thigh cutlets, fat trimmed
1 brown onion, halved, chopped
1 carrot, peeled, chopped
1 celery stick, trimmed, chopped
2 garlic cloves, chopped
2 tablespoon parsley stems, chopped
6 sprigs fresh thyme, leaves picked
8 cups of water
½ teaspoon whole black peppercorns
Salt flakes
¼ cup fresh parsley, chopped

Preparation
Add the chicken, peppercorns, water, thyme, parsley, garlic, celery, carrots and onion to a saucepan and then cook the mixture to a boil. Reduce its heat, cover and cook for 40 minutes. Discard the chicken bones, shred them, and return to the soup. Garnish with parsley and serve warm.

Shorabat Addas

Preparation time: 5 minutes
Cook time: 60 minutes
Nutrition facts (per serving): 345 Cal (21g fat, 26g protein, 2g fiber)

This rich Lebanese Shorabat Addas is a typical Lebanese entree, which is a must to have on a healthy menu. It has this rich mix of onion, green lentils, and tomato paste.

Ingredients (8 servings)
Shorabat Addas
2 tablespoon grass-fed butter
1 medium onion, chopped
2 garlic cloves, minced
2 carrots, chopped
1 celery stalk, chopped
1 cup green lentils, soaked overnight
6 cups chicken broth
1 tablespoon tomato paste
1 teaspoon cumin
Sea salt, to taste
Black pepper, to taste

Garnish
Olive oil
Lemon wedges

Preparation
Sauté the carrots, celery, garlic, and onion with olive oil in a skillet until soft. Stir in the black pepper, salt, broth, lentils, cumin, and tomato paste. Cook the lentils for 60 minutes on medium heat. Garnish with lemon juice and olive oil. Serve warm.

Lebanese Lentil Chard Soup (Adas bi Hamoud)

Preparation time: 10 minutes
Cook time: 35 minutes
Nutrition facts (per serving): 117 Cal (1g fat, 5g protein, 2g fiber)

The lentil chard soup is made from a mixture of potato, chard and lentils. You can serve this soup with your favorite crusted bread.

Ingredients (4 servings)
¼ cup brown lentils
3 cups of filtered water
1 medium potato, diced
1 medium yellow onion, diced
1 teaspoon salt
1 teaspoon sumac
2 handfuls chard, chopped
Black pepper, to taste
1 lemon, juiced
Lemon wedges and black pepper, to serve

Preparation
Add the lentils, water, potato, chard stems, and onion to a cooking pot. Cook this mixture to a boil, reduce its heat, cover and cook for 35 minutes. Stir in the chard leaves, black pepper, and salt. Garnish with lemon wedges. Serve warm.

Barley Soup
(Ash-e-jow)

Preparation time: 10 minutes
Cook time: 1 hour 31 minutes
Nutrition facts (per serving): 330 Cal (29g fat, 7g protein, 3g fiber)

Try this Lebanese barley soup with your favorite herbs on top. Adding a dollop of cream or yogurt will make it even richer in taste.

Ingredients (8 servings)

2 quarts chicken stock
2 tablespoon olive oil
1 medium onion, diced
1 cup uncooked pearl barley
1 teaspoon turmeric
1 lime, juiced
¼ cup tomato paste
Salt, to taste
Black pepper, to taste
1 cup carrots, diced
½ cup sour cream
½ cup fresh parsley, chopped
8 lime wedges

Preparation

Sauté the onion with oil in a soup pot until soft. Stir in the pearl barley and sauté for 1 minute. Stir in the chicken stock, black pepper, salt, tomato paste, lime juice, and turmeric, then cook the mixture to a boil, reduce its heat, and cook for 1 hour on a simmer. Add the carrots and cook for 30 minutes with occasional stirring. Mix the sour cream with ½ cup of the soup mixture in a bowl and return to the soup. Mix well and garnish with lime wedges and parsley. Serve warm.

Red Vermicelli Soup

Preparation time: 10 minutes
Cook time: 5 minutes
Nutrition facts (per serving): 125 Cal (4g fat, 14g protein, 3g fiber)

Enjoy this red vermicelli soup with crispy bread and a fresh vegetable salad on the side. The warming bowl of this soup makes a great serving for all the special dinners.

Ingredients (4 servings)
1 cup of vermicelli
3 tablespoon of tomato sauce
3 tablespoon of olive oil
¼ bundle of parsley, chopped
Salt and 7 spices, to taste
2 cups of water

Preparation
Sauté the vermicelli with 3 tablespoon olive oil in a cooking pot until golden brown. Stir in the water and the rest of the ingredients. Mix and cook until the mixture boils. Cook for 5 minutes with occasional stirring and garnish with parsley. Serve warm.

Chicken Dumpling Soup

Preparation time: 15 minutes
Cook time: 66 minutes
Nutrition facts (per serving): 241 Cal (15g fat, 22g protein, 4g fiber)

You cannot expect to have Lebanese cuisine and not try the traditional chicken dumpling soup in it. This soup is full of spices, beans, and chicken.

Ingredients (6 servings)
1 tablespoon olive oil
2 tablespoon butter
¼ cup hazelnuts roasted, peeled, crushed
1 tablespoon red Aleppo pepper
1 lemon, zested

Black cabbage and white bean soup
3 ½ oz. dried cannellini beans, soaked
2 tablespoon butter
1 brown onion, chopped
1 corn cob, kernels removed
1 oz. tomato paste
3 ½ oz. fine cornmeal
1 bunch black cabbage, leaves, shredded
Salt, to taste
2 lemons, juiced

Chicken dumplings
3 ½ oz. corn bread, crumbled
3 ½ oz. chicken mince
1 egg white
¼ cup flat-leaf parsley, chopped
1 pinch of red Aleppo pepper
Salt, to taste

Preparation

Add the beans and water to a cooking pot and cook for 30 minutes on a simmer until soft. Drain the cooked beans. Sauté the corn and the onion with the butter in a saucepan for 6 minutes. Stir in the tomatoes, beans, 8 ½ cup of water, and cook for 25 minutes on low heat. Stir in the cabbages and the lemon juice. Mix all the ingredients for the dumplings in a bowl and make small balls from this mixture. Add the dumplings to a pan, greased with butter. Sear the dumplings for 3 minutes per side. Transfer the dumplings to the soup and cook for 5 minutes. Stir in the rest of the ingredients and serve warm.

Pomegranate Soup
(Ashe-e-anar)

Preparation time: 15 minutes
Cook time: 1 hour 55 minutes
Nutrition facts (per serving): 455 Cal (9g fat, 39g protein, 2g fiber)

Loaded with lots of flavor, Pomegranate soup is a Lebanese lamb lentils entrée that makes an amazing serving for all your meals. Enjoy it warm with your favorite bread.

Ingredients (8 servings)
2 cups parsley, chopped
1 cup mint, chopped
1 beet, peeled and chopped
1 cup red lentils
1 cup of rice
1 lb. lamb shanks
4 cups pomegranate juice
⅔ cups pomegranate molasses
⅓ cup sugar
2 tablespoon angelica seeds

Preparation
Sauté the onions with oil in a skillet until caramelized. Stir in the turmeric, garlic, and meat, then sauté for 5 minutes. Add 2 quarts of water and cook the meat on a simmer for 1 hour until the meat is tender. Stir in the lentils and rice and then cook for 25 minutes. Add the pomegranate juice and herbs. Then cook for another 25 minutes. Garnish with the pomegranate arils, herbs, and sliced onions. Serve warm.

Harira Soup

Preparation time: 10 minutes
Cook time: 28 minutes
Nutrition facts (per serving): 141 Cal (6g fat, 4.7g protein, 1.2g fiber)

Try this super tasty Lebanese Harira soup prepared with lamb, onion, lots of seasoning, etc. Serve it to your family to make your meals special, and you'll never stop having it; that's how heavenly the combination tastes.

Ingredients (8 servings)
Soup
7 oz. boneless lamb diced
1 oz. corn oil
5 oz. onion, small diced
3 ½ oz. ginger, minced
3 ½ oz. tomato pronto
8 cups water
3 tablespoon chicken bouillon powder
3 ½ oz. spaghetti pasta
⅔ oz. tomato paste
⅔ oz. turmeric powder
⅔ oz. cumin powder
⅓ oz. lime seasoning powder
3 ½ oz. lentil green, boiled, drained

Garnish
Lime seasoning powder
2 ½ tablespoon coriander leaves

Preparation
Sauté the onion and ginger with oil in a saucepan for 3 minutes. Stir in the lamb cubes and sauté until brown. Stir in the water, chicken bouillon

powder, water, tomato paste, and tomato pronto. Boil this mixture then reduce the heat and cook for 10 minutes. Stir in the cumin, turmeric, chickpeas, and lentils and then cook for 10 minutes with occasional stirring. Mix the lime seasoning with water in a bowl. Pour into the soup and garnish with coriander. Serve warm.

Main Dishes

Lamb Shawarma

Preparation time: 10 minutes
Cook time: 3 hours 30 minutes
Nutrition facts (per serving): 272 Cal (16g fat, 22g protein, 1g fiber)

If you haven't tried the Lebanese lamb shawarma before, then here comes a simple and easy to cook recipe that you can recreate at home in no time with minimum effort.

Ingredients (8 servings)
4 lbs. lamb shoulder (bone-in)

Shawarma Paste
3 garlic cloves, minced
1 tablespoon ground coriander
1 tablespoon ground cumin
1 tablespoon ground cardamom
1 teaspoon cayenne pepper
2 teaspoons smoked paprika
1 ½ teaspoon salt
½ teaspoon black pepper
¼ cup olive oil
3 tablespoon lemon juice
2 cups of water

Preparation
At 350 degrees F, preheat your oven. Mix all the paste ingredients in a bowl. Rub this paste over the lamb liberally. Place the prepared lamb in a roasting pan, cover, and marinate for 24 hours. Pour a little water around the lamb, cover with the foil, and roast for 3 hours in the oven. Remove the foil, brush it with cooking juices, and bake for 30 minutes. Serve warm.

Lebanese Lamb Stew with Eggplant

Preparation time: 15 minutes
Cook time: 8 hours 30 minutes
Nutrition facts (per serving): 363 Cal (10g fat, 29g protein, 0g fiber)

This Lebanese lamb stew with eggplant is a healthy entrée that can be served with some coleslaw on the side, which will enhance its flavor and will make it more nutritious.

Ingredients (4 servings)
1 large eggplant, cut into cubes
6 tablespoon olive oil
1 lb. lamb, boneless and cubed
1 large onion, diced
3 garlic cloves, minced
½ cup red wine
3 tablespoon tomato paste
14 oz. canned tomatoes, chopped
2 cups lamb stock
1 bay leaf
2 teaspoon black pepper
1 teaspoon thyme
1 teaspoon ground cinnamon
½ teaspoon allspice, ground
½ teaspoon nutmeg, grated
1 teaspoon salt
Parsley to finish, chopped

Preparation
At 400 degrees F, preheat your oven. Toss the eggplant cubes with 2 tablespoon olive oil in a baking sheet and roast for 20 minutes. Sauté lamb with 2 tablespoon olive oil in a skillet until brown. Stir in garlic and onions

and then sauté for 2 minutes. Transfer all the ingredients to a slow cooker, cover the lid, and cook for 8 hours on low heat. Garnish with parsley and serve warm.

Eggplant Fetteh

Preparation time: 10 minutes
Cook time: 50 minutes
Nutrition facts (per serving): 324 Cal (16g fat, 9g protein, 14g fiber)

Let's make quick Aubergine or eggplant Fetteh with these simple ingredients. Mix them together and then cook to yield great flavors.

Ingredients (6 servings)
4 eggplant, peeled and sliced
4 ounces (120 ml) olive oil
1½ (100 g) thin pita, fresh
2 garlic cloves, finely sliced
1 teaspoon Aleppo chili flakes
10 ounces (300 g) natural yogurt
2 teaspoon lemon juice
2 tomatoes, grated
2 tablespoons mint leaves, torn
Black pepper, to taste
Salt, to taste
Pomegranate seeds to garnish

Preparation
At 428 degrees F, preheat your oven. Spread all the eggplant slices in a baking tray lined with parchment paper in a single layer. Drizzle 4 tablespoons oil, salt, and black pepper over the slices and roast them for 30 minutes in the oven until brown and soft. Allow the slices to cool and switch the oven heat to 350 degrees F. Split the pitta into two parts and roll each half. Slice these rolls into 3 mm wide strips. Toss the strips with 2 tablespoon oil, black pepper, and ⅛th salt in a bowl. Spread these strips in a baking tray and bake for 10 minutes until golden brown. Add 2 tablespoon oil to a small saucepan and place it over medium-high heat. Stir in the chili flakes and garlic and

then sauté for 3 minutes. Transfer to a bowl. Add the yogurt and cook for 5 minutes. Stir in the lemon juice, eggplant, ¼ teaspoon salt, and 4 tablespoons water and cook for 5 minutes with occasional stirring. Transfer the prepared eggplant mixture to a serving bowl. Top it with mint and tomato. Garnish with toasted pita, pomegranate seeds, and garlic oil. Serve.

Lebanese Lamb Rice

Preparation time: 15 minutes
Cook time: 31 minutes
Nutrition facts (per serving): 351 Cal (16g fat, 45g protein, 18g fiber)

Have you tried Lebanese lamb rice before? Well, here's a Lebanese delight that can add lamb meat and rice to your dinner table in a delicious way.

Ingredients (4 servings)
1 tablespoon ghee
1 lb. ground lamb
½ teaspoon salt
½ teaspoon black pepper
1 cup dry basmati rice
2 cups bone broth
¼ cup raw shelled pistachios,
1 tablespoon fresh mint leaves, chopped

Servings
1 cup yogurt
Fresh cucumber slices

Preparation
Sauté the lamb with ghee in a skillet for 10 minutes until brown. Stir in the rice and sauté for 1 minute. Stir in stock, cover and cook for 20 minutes on low heat. Garnish with mint and pistachios. Garnish with yogurt and cucumber slices. Serve.

Lamb Stew

Preparation time: 10 minutes
Cook time: 25 minutes
Nutrition facts (per serving): 271 Cal (9g fat, 23g protein, 6g fiber)

Here's a simple Lebanese lamb stew recipe made with some basic ingredients. Serve this with some warm bread or rice.

Ingredients (4 servings)
1 lb. lamb cubes
1 onion chopped
1 potato cut into cubes
3 garlic cloves minced
¼ cup tomato paste
Salt, to taste
2 cups hot water
3 whole cardamom
¼ teaspoon cinnamon powder
3 whole cloves
½ teaspoon cumin
1 ½ tablespoon Yamani spice mix
Oil

Preparation
Sauté the onion with oil in a pressure cooker until soft. Stir in the lamb and sauté until brown. Add garlic and spices and then sauté for 1 minute. Add water and tomato paste and then cook the mixture to boil. Add the potatoes, cover with a pressure-cooking lid, and cook for 15 minutes on low heat. Once done, release the pressure completely then remove the lid. Mix well and serve warm.

Barbecued Lamb with Lebanese Garlic Sauce

Preparation time: 10 minutes
Cook time: 60 minutes
Nutrition facts (per serving): 456 Cal (33g fat, 41g protein, 2g fiber)

This barbecued lamb with garlic sauce is known as the classic Lebanese dinner. The lamb shoulder with thick garlic sauce tastes heavenly with rice and bread.

Ingredients (4 servings)
2 ½ lbs. boned lamb shoulder
2 teaspoon allspice
⅓ cup olive oil
1 baby cos lettuce heart, trimmed, leaves separated
14 oz. tomato medley mix halved
1 Lebanese cucumber, halved, sliced
½ small red onion, sliced
½ cup torn fresh mint leaves
¼ cup lemon juice
Lebanese bread, warmed, to serve

Lebanese Garlic Sauce
6 garlic cloves, peeled, chopped
1 teaspoon sea salt
¼ cup lemon juice
1 egg white
1 cup rice bran oil
2 tablespoon iced water

Preparation
Mix the lamb with ¼ cup oil and allspice in a ceramic dish. Cover and refrigerate the meat for 2 hours. Mix the garlic with lemon juice and salt in

a food processor. Add the egg white and mix well. Pour in the oil and continue blending. Slowly pour in iced water and continue mixing until fluffy. Transfer the mixture to a bowl, cover, and refrigerate. Set a barbecue grill over medium-low heat and grill the lamb for 15 minutes. Flip and cover the lamb for 35 minutes. Transfer the lamb to a plate, cover and leave for 10 minutes. Mix the onion, mint, cucumber, tomato, and lettuce in a bowl. Stir in the remaining oil, lemon juice, black pepper, and salt. Slice the cooked lamb and serve with the garlic sauce and salad. Enjoy.

Middle Eastern Lamb Kofta

Preparation time: 10 minutes
Cook time: 14 minutes
Nutrition facts (per serving): 515 Cal (27g fat, 29g protein, 1.2g fiber)

Eastern Lamb Kofta offers another popular entrée that's known for its rich, meaty flavor. Serve them with toasted burgers and salad.

Ingredients (8 servings)
¼ cup pine nuts
¼ cup almonds
¼ cup walnuts
1 small yellow onion, chopped
3 Garlic cloves, chopped
1 small red bell pepper, chopped
1 small jalapeño pepper, chopped
½ cup cilantro leaves
2 pounds ground lamb
¾ teaspoon ground cumin
¼ teaspoon ground cinnamon
¼ teaspoon ground cardamom
¼ teaspoon ground cloves
1 ½ teaspoon salt
¼ teaspoon white pepper
Tzatziki and hummus, for serving

Preparation
Blend nuts in a food processor until chopped. Roast the nuts in a dry skillet over medium heat for 6 minutes. Transfer them to a bowl and stir in the rest of the ingredients. Pulse this mixture in a food processor. Make 2 inch round and ½ inch thick patties from this mixture and place them in a greased baking sheet. Cover and refrigerate them until set. Grease a grill and preheat

at medium-high heat. Grill the patties for 4 minutes per side. Serve warm with hummus and tzatziki. Enjoy.

Lamb Pilaf

Preparation time: 15 minutes
Cook time: 2 hours 58 minutes
Nutrition facts (per serving): 386 Cal (15g fat, 31g protein, 1g fiber)

If you haven't tried the famous lamb shoulder with sausages, apricots and lentils before, then here comes a simple and easy to cook recipe that you can recreate at home in no time with minimum effort.

Ingredients (8 servings)
4 tablespoon olive oil
2 lbs. lamb shoulder, diced
10 ½ oz. merguez sausages, chopped
2 red onions, sliced
3 garlic cloves, chopped
2 carrots, sliced
½ teaspoon ground cinnamon
½ teaspoon paprika
1 teaspoon ground cumin
½ teaspoon cumin seeds
1 teaspoon ground turmeric
4 ½ oz. dried apricots halved
4 cups chicken stock
10 ½ oz. long-grain white rice
1 ⅔ oz. dried lentils, rinsed
1 handful of parsley, chopped

Preparation
At 325 degrees F, preheat your oven. Sear the lamb meat in a skillet with ½ of the oil for 4 minutes per side until brown. Transfer the brown meat to a plate. Stir in the remaining oil, carrots, garlic, and onions and then sauté for 5 minutes. Add the spices and mix well. Return the lamb and add stock,

seasoning and apricots. Cover and cook for 2 hours in the oven. Add the sausages, lentils, and rice, cover, and cook for 45 minutes in the oven. Garnish with parsley and serve warm.

Lebanese Lamb Tacos

Preparation time: 10 minutes
Cook time: 3 hours 13 minutes
Nutrition facts (per serving): 532 Cal (28g fat, 270 protein, 1g fiber)

Make these lamb tacos at home in no time and enjoy with some garnish on top. Adding a drizzle of paprika makes them super tasty.

Ingredients (4 servings)
Lamb Shoulder
4 pound lamb shoulder, boneless
3 teaspoon salt
1 teaspoon black pepper
1 teaspoon paprika
2 teaspoon 7 spices mix
1 teaspoon sumac
1 teaspoon garlic powder
10 garlic cloves, peeled and trimmed
2 tablespoon toum, or olive oil
2 onions, sliced
1 cup red wine
Juice of 2 lemons
1 tra dollop of toum
2 tablespoon olive oil

Cabbage Beet Slaw
2 cloves of fresh garlic
1 teaspoon salt
1 teaspoon pomegranate molasses
2 whole lemons, juiced
1 cup yogurt or sour cream
2 cups shredded cabbage

1 whole fresh beet, peeled and sliced

Taco Ingredients
Pita bread, fresh
Feta cheese
Thick yogurt
Scallions

Preparation
At 325 degrees F, preheat your oven. Spread the lamb on a baking sheet. Mix the garlic powder, seven spices, sumac, paprika, black pepper, and salt, then rub over the lamb. Add the garlic cloves and oil around the lamb. Sauté the onion with oil in a pot for 5 minutes. Add the lamb and cook for 4 minutes per side. Add the toum, lemon juice, and cooking liquid. Cover and cook for 3 hours in the oven. Meanwhile, mix all the islaw ingredients in a bowl. Serve warm with slaw.

Lebanese Chicken With 7-Spice

Preparation time: 15 minutes
Cook time: 50 minutes
Nutrition facts (per serving): 236 Cal (17g fat, 29 protein, 2g fiber)

This quick and easy chicken with 7 spices recipe is also quite famous in the region; in fact, it's a must to try because of its nutritional content.

Ingredients (4 servings)
2 lbs. chicken, bone-in thighs
2 tablespoon olive oil
2 ½ teaspoon salt
2 teaspoon black pepper
2 tablespoon Lebanese 7-spices
1 red onion, sliced
4 garlic cloves, chopped
1 tablespoon preserved lemon, chopped
1 lemon, sliced
¼ cup Marcona almonds, slivered
Parsley for garnish

Seven Spice Recipe
1 teaspoon cumin
1 teaspoon allspice
1 teaspoon cinnamon
1 teaspoon coriander
½ teaspoon ground cloves
½ teaspoon nutmeg
¼ teaspoon cardamom

Preparation

At 400 degrees F, preheat your oven. Mix the chicken with the 7 spice, salt, and olive oil in a bowl. Add the lemon slices, preserved lemon, garlic, and onion and then mix well. Layer a baking sheet with parchment paper. Add the meat to the baking sheet, bake for 45 minutes, and then broil for 5 minutes. Toast the almonds with olive oil in a skillet until golden brown. Garnish the meat with the almonds. Drizzle black pepper and salt. Serve warm.

Shish Tawook Chicken

Preparation time: 10 minutes
Cook time: 7 minutes
Nutrition facts (per serving): 388 Cal (11g fat, 28g protein, 3g fiber)

This Lebanese shisk tawook chicken is everything you must be looking for to make your dinner loaded with nutrients. The combination of chicken with spices delivers a complete package with a mixed greens salad.

Ingredients (2 servings)
20 oz. boneless chicken breasts, cubed
1 juice and zest of lemon
2 garlic cloves, grated
1 teaspoon salt
½ teaspoon black pepper
1 tablespoon olive oil
Fresh parsley, to serve

Preparation
Mix the chicken cubes with black pepper, salt, garlic, zest, and lemon juice in a bowl. Cover and marinate the chicken in the refrigerator for 20 minutes. Add the oil to a suitable skillet and heat over medium-high heat. Sauté the chicken in the skillet for 7 minutes. Garnish with parsley and serve warm.

Chicken Shawarma
(Middle Eastern)

Preparation time: 15 minutes
Cook time: 10 minutes
Nutrition facts (per serving): 519 Cal (12g fat, 20g protein, 2g fiber)

This Lebanese chicken shawarma is loved by all, young and adult. It's simple and quick to make. This delight is great to serve at dinner tables.

Ingredients (4 servings)
2 lbs. chicken thigh fillets, boneless

Marinade
1 garlic clove, minced
1 tablespoon ground coriander
1 tablespoon ground cumin
1 tablespoon ground cardamom
1 teaspoon ground cayenne pepper
2 teaspoons smoked paprika
2 teaspoon salt
Black pepper, to taste
2 tablespoon lemon juice
3 tablespoon olive oil

Yoghurt Sauce
1 cup Greek yogurt
1 garlic clove , crushed
1 teaspoon cumin
A squeeze of lemon juice
Salt and black pepper, to taste

Servings

6 Lebanese pita bread
Sliced lettuce
Tomato slices

Preparation

Mix the chicken with all the marinade ingredients in a bowl. Cover and marinate the chicken in the refrigerator for 24 hours. Set a grill over medium-high heat. Grease the grilling grate with cooking spray. Grill the marinated chicken for 5 minutes per side. Allow the chicken to cool. Cut the chicken into thin slices. Mix all the yogurt ingredients in a bowl. Place the flatbreads on the working surface and divide the yogurt sauce on top. Add the vegetables and the chicken on top. Roll the flatbread and serve.

Lebanese Chicken Wraps

Preparation time: 10 minutes
Cook time: 12 minutes
Nutrition facts (per serving): 566 Cal (43g fat, 26g protein, 0.8g fiber)

Here comes the famous Lebanese chicken wraps, which is made from the chicken breast and pine nuts topping.

Ingredients (4 servings)
4 skinless chicken breasts
7 oz. Greek yogurt
Juice and zest 1 lemon
1 teaspoon allspice
2 teaspoon olive oil
2 garlic cloves, crushed
½ oz. pine nuts, toasted
1 small bunch parsley, chopped
2 tomatoes, diced
½ cucumber, diced
4 tortilla wraps
Mixed salad, to serve

Preparation
Place the chicken breasts in a baking sheet lined with parchment paper. Cover with another parchment paper and flatten it with a rolling pin. Mix half of the yogurt with salt, garlic, olive oil, allspice, lemon zest, and lemon juice in a large bowl. Add chicken to this mixture, coat, cover, and refrigerate for 30 minutes. Set a griddle pan over high heat and sear the chicken for 6 minutes per side. Place the tortilla wraps on the working surface and add the yogurt, pine nuts, chicken, tomatoes, cucumber, and parsley on top of the wraps. Add lemon juice on top, wrap, and toast the rolls on the griddle pan. Serve with mixed salad.

Lebanese Chicken Fatteh

Preparation time: 15 minutes
Cook time: 32 minutes
Nutrition facts (per serving): 722 Cal (57g fat, 36g protein, 4g fiber)

The famous Lebanese chicken fatteh is a must to try on the Lebanese menu. Try cooking it at home with these healthy ingredients and enjoy.

Ingredients (4 servings)
4 bone-in chicken breasts
Salt, to taste
1 tablespoon apple cider vinegar
2 dried bay leaves
2 cinnamon sticks
4 whole cardamom pods, crushed
6 cloves
Water
Olive oil
1 medium yellow onion, peeled, and sliced
3 garlic cloves, crushed
1 teaspoon sweet Spanish paprika
1 teaspoon ground sumac
½ cup toasted pine nuts
½ cup toasted almonds sliced
Parsley leaves for garnish
2 loaves Lebanese pita bread, toasted, and broken into chips

Mint Yogurt Sauce
1 ½ cup yogurt
2 garlic cloves, crushed
½ cup fresh mint, chopped
1 pinch salt

Preparation

Mix all the ingredients for the mint yogurt sauce in a bowl. Cover and refrigerate this sauce. Add the chicken, enough water to cover, the cinnamon sticks, cardamom, bay leaves, salt, and apple cider vinegar. Cover, cook for 20 minutes, and then drain. Cut the chicken into cubes. Sauté onions with oil in a skillet for 4 minutes. Stir in garlic and sauté for 30 seconds. Add the chicken, sumac, and paprika and then sauté for 7 minutes. Stir in the toasted nuts and garnish with parsley leaves. Serve the chicken on top of the pita bread and garnish with the yogurt sauce.

Herb and Garlic Chicken

Preparation time: 10 minutes
Cook time: 14 minutes
Nutrition facts (per serving): 303 Cal (18g fat, 14g protein, 0.4g fiber)

If you want something exotic and delicious on your dinner menu, then nothing can taste better than this Lebanese herb and garlic chicken.

Ingredients (6 servings)
6 boneless chicken thighs
6 garlic cloves, grated
Juice and zest of 2 lemons
3 tablespoon olive oil
2 tablespoon fresh parsley, minced
2 tablespoon fresh mint, minced
1 tablespoon fresh thyme, minced
1 tablespoon fresh oregano, minced
1 ½ teaspoon salt
1 tablespoon sesame seeds
¾ teaspoon sumac
⅔ cup plain Greek yogurt
¼ teaspoon black pepper

Preparation
Mix the garlic with the lemon juice, lemon zest, sesame seeds, sumac, 1 ½ teaspoon salt, oregano, thyme, mint, parsley, and oil in a bowl. Add the chicken to this mixture, mix well, cover, and refrigerate for 30 minutes. Preheat a grill over high heat. Grill the chicken or 7 minutes per side. Mix the yogurt with the rest of the ingredients in a bowl. Pour the yogurt over the chicken and serve warm.

Lebanese Chicken and Potatoes

Preparation time: 15 minutes
Cook time: 48 minutes
Nutrition facts (per serving): 337 Cal (18g fat, 28g protein, 2g fiber)

If you haven't tried the famous Lebanese chicken and potatoes before, then here comes a simple and easy to cook recipe that you can recreate at home in no time with minimum efforts.

Ingredients (4 servings)
2 tablespoon olive oil
3 potatoes, sliced
4 lemons, juiced
10 garlic cloves, crushed
1 chicken bouillon cube, mixed with ½ cup hot water
¼ cup olive oil
1 teaspoon seven spice powder
½ teaspoon salt
¼ teaspoon black pepper
6 chicken breasts, sliced
8 garlic cloves, whole and peeled

Preparation
At 390 degrees F, preheat your oven. Sauté the potatoes with oil in a large skillet for 4 minutes per side. Mix the lemon juice, black pepper, salt, seven spice, olive oil, water, stock cubes, and garlic in a bowl. Place the chicken in a baking dish and pour half of the sauce over the mixture. Add the garlic cloves and the potato slices around the chicken. Pour remaining sauce on top, cover with a foil and bake for 30 minutes in the oven. Flip the chicken and bake for 10 minutes. Serve warm.

Chargrilled Garlic Chicken (Farrouj Meshwi)

Preparation time: 15 minutes
Cook time: 35 minutes
Nutrition facts (per serving): 338 Cal (9g fat, 28g protein, 0g fiber)

The chicken tastes great when seasoned with special sumac marinade. Adding the special Lebanese garlic sauce to the chicken makes it soft, moist, and juicy.

Ingredients (6 servings)
1 whole chicken, butterflied
¼ cup toum (Lebanese garlic sauce)

Marinade
½ teaspoon cayenne pepper
1½ teaspoon paprika
1 teaspoon ground cumin
1 tablespoon Sumac
⅛ teaspoon ground cinnamon
6 garlic cloves, crushed
⅓ cup lemon juice
⅓ cup olive oil

Preparation
Mix the chicken marinade in a bowl. Rub this marinade over the chicken and place it on a baking sheet. Cover and refrigerate overnight. At 400 degrees F, preheat your oven. Roast the chicken for 25 minutes. Flip the chicken after every 10 minutes. Cut into pieces and serve warm with bread, pickles, and toum.

Sayadieh

Preparation time: 5 minutes
Cook time: 45 minutes
Nutrition facts (per serving): 424 Cal (21g fat, 21g protein, 1g fiber)

The Lebanese Sayadieh is loved by all due to its amazing blend of onion, rice, and fish cod. This meal makes an irresistible serving for the table.

Ingredients (4 servings)
Onions and the rice
3 tablespoon olive oil
4 onions, sliced
1 teaspoon cumin powder
½ teaspoon turmeric powder
½ teaspoon cinnamon powder
1 ½ teaspoon salt
½ teaspoon black pepper powder
4 cups of water
1 tablespoon tomato paste
2 cups basmati rice, soaked

Fish
2 tablespoon olive oil
1 ½ lbs. white fish cod, cut into pieces
1 teaspoon cumin powder
½ teaspoon paprika powder
1 pinch each Salt and black pepper

Garnish
Toasted pine nuts or almond slivers
Fresh parsley, chopped

Preparation

Sauté an onion with oil in a large pot over medium-high heat for 15 minutes. Blend the onions with cumin, 1 cup water, turmeric, black pepper, salt, cinnamon, and tomato paste in a blender until smooth. Pour this sauce into a saucepan and add the remaining 3 cups of water and rice. Boil this mixture, cover, and cook for 20 minutes on low heat. Sear the fish in a skillet, greased with cooking oil. Drizzle the spices over the fish and cook for 5 minutes per side. Add the fish to the rice and garnish with parsley, nuts, and caramelized onion. Serve warm.

Lebanese Fish with Tahini Sauce

Preparation time: 15 minutes
Cook time: 30 minutes
Nutrition facts (per serving): 261 Cal (22g fat, 14 protein, 2g fiber)

This Lebanese fish with tahini sauce is a must to have on this Lebanese menu. It has an easy mix of rice, tahini sauce, and fish.

Ingredients (4 servings)
Tahini sauce and the rice
1 garlic cloves, minced
1 bunch flat-leaf parsley
¾ cup tahini
⅓ cup lemon juice
¾ cup water
1 pinch salt
1 cup basmati rice
4 tablespoon unsalted butter
2 tablespoon olive oil
1 yellow onion, peeled and sliced
½ cup pine nuts

Fish and the assembly
2 pounds fish filets (halibut, hake or any white-fleshed)
2 tablespoon olive oil
1 pinch Salt and black pepper
2 tablespoon butter
2 limes, quartered
½ bunch cilantro, chopped

Preparation

Blend the garlic with the parsley in a food processor, add tahini, and then blend. Stir in the lemon juice, a pinch of salt, a drizzle of water, and then mix well. Sauté the onion with the butter, oil, and a pinch of salt in a skillet until brown. Transfer the onion to a plate. Stir in the pine nuts and sauté until golden brown. Boil the water with salt in a cooking pot and stir in rice. Cook 10 minutes, then drain. Rub the fish with olive oil, black pepper, and salt. Sear the fish in the greased skillet for 5 minutes per side. Mix the rice with 2 tablespoon butter, pine nuts, and onions in a bowl. Spread the rice on a serving platter. Place the fish on top of the rice. Garnish with pine nuts and lime slices. Serve warm.

Shakshuka Fish Style

Preparation time: 15 minutes
Cook time: 29 minutes
Nutrition facts (per serving): 493 Cal (15g fat, 30g protein, 1.7g fiber)

A perfect mix of fish fillets with the delicious shakshuka base is a must to try. Serve warm with your favorite side salad for the best taste.

Ingredients (4 servings)
Cod fillet, medium size
2 teaspoon ground coriander
2 teaspoon sumac
1 ½ teaspoon ground cumin
1 teaspoon dill weed
1 teaspoon turmeric
1 large sweet onion, chopped
Olive Oil
8 garlic cloves, chopped
1 jalapeno peppers, chopped
5 medium ripe tomatoes, diced or chopped
3 tablespoon tomato paste
1 lime, juice of
½ cup water
Salt and black pepper, to taste
2 lbs. cod fillet, cut into pieces
½ cup fresh parsley, chopped
1 tablespoon fresh mint leaves, chopped

Preparation
Mix the turmeric with the dill, cumin, sumac, and coriander in a bowl. Sauté the onions with 2 tablespoon oil in a skillet for 2 minutes. Stir in the jalapeno and garlic and then sauté for 2 minutes. Stir in the tomatoes and ½ of the

spice mixture. Stir in the black pepper, salt, water, lime juice, and tomato paste. Mix well, cover, and cook for 10 minutes with occasional stirring. Place the fish in the tomato mixture, cover, and cook for 15 minutes. Garnish with mint leaves and parsley. Serve warm.

Lebanese Baked Fish

Preparation time: 15 minutes
Cook time: 47 minutes
Nutrition facts (per serving): 357 Cal (10g fat, 13g protein, 2g fiber)

The Lebanese baked sea bream fish with tahini sauce is famous for its unique taste and aroma, and now you can bring those exotic flavors home by using this recipe.

Ingredients (8 servings)
4 lbs. sea bream fish

Tatbileh filling
2 green chilis, chopped
5 garlic cloves, crushed
¼ cup lemon juice
Slices of 2 lemons
1 tablespoon lemon rind
1 tablespoon cumin
1 tablespoon olive oil
Salt and black pepper, to taste

Rub
¼ cup cooking oil
1 teaspoon coriander
1 teaspoon cayenne pepper
Salt and black pepper, to taste

Tahini sauce
1 medium onion, chopped
2 tablespoon cooking oil
10 garlic cloves, crushed

2 tablespoon coriander powder
1 cup tahini
2 cups water
1 cup lemon juice
½ cup walnuts, chopped
Salt and black pepper, to taste
Red chili flakes, crushed

Garnish
Fried almonds, to taste
Red chili, to taste
Pine nuts, to taste
Chopped coriander, to taste

Preparation
Mix all the rub ingredients in a bowl and rub over the fish liberally. Mix all the filling ingredients in a bowl. Stuff the fish with the prepared filling and cover to marinate for 15 minutes. Cover the fish with a foil sheet and bake for 20 minutes. Sauté the onions with 2 tablespoon oil in a skillet until soft. Stir in the garlic and sauté for 2 minutes. Add the walnuts, red chili flakes, black pepper, salt, tahini sauce, and coriander and then cook for 10 minutes. Pour the sauce over the fish and garnish with red chili, coriander, pine nuts, and almonds. Serve warm.

Lebanese Spicy Fish (Samke Harra)

Preparation time: 10 minutes
Cook time: 28 minutes
Nutrition facts (per serving): 428 Cal (18g fat, 26g protein, 1g fiber)

Have you tried the Lebanese spicy fish before? Well, now you can enjoy this unique and flavorsome combination by cooking this recipe at home.

Ingredients (2 servings)
1 whole red snapper, cleaned
1 teaspoon salt
½ teaspoon black pepper, ground
2 teaspoon harissa paste
½ teaspoon urfa biber pepper, crushed
4 lemon slices

Tartar Sauce
¼ cup olive oil
½ sweet onion, diced
8 garlic cloves, chopped
1 green pepper, diced
1 jalapeño pepper, diced
1 serrano pepper, diced
2 medium tomatoes, diced
1 teaspoon allspice, ground
½ teaspoon coriander, ground
½ teaspoon cumin, ground
½ teaspoon Aleppo pepper, crushed
Salt and black pepper, to taste
½ teaspoon cayenne pepper, ground
1 cup tahini

Juice of 2 lemons
1 cup Greek yogurt, full fat optional
1 handful of fresh parsley, chopped
1 handful of fresh cilantro, chopped
¼ cup toasted pine nuts, for garnish

Preparation

At 400 degrees F, preheat your oven. Place the fish on a suitable baking sheet. Rub the fish with harissa and stuff with lemons. Drizzle chili, black pepper, and salt on top. Bake the fish for 20 minutes in the oven. Sauté the onion with the oil in a skillet until soft. Stir in the green pepper, serrano, jalapeno, and garlic and then sauté for 8 minutes. Stir in the allspice and mix well. Mix the tahini with the lemon and pour into the skillet. Mix well and pour this sauce over the fish. Garnish with herbs and nuts. Serve warm.

Baba Ganouj

Preparation time: 15 minutes
Cook time: 20 minutes
Nutrition facts (per serving): 212 Cal (9g fat, 17g protein, 0.5g fiber)

The famous baba Ganouj recipe is here to make your Lebanese cuisine extra special. Make it with roasted eggplant slices for the best taste.

Ingredients (6 servings)

1 big eggplant, peeled and sliced
1 medium tomato, chopped
½ cup packed parsley, chopped
3 tablespoons pomegranate concentrate
⅓ cup pomegranate seeds
2 cloves mashed garlic
A dash of cumin
2 tablespoons olive oil
Salt and black pepper, to taste

Preparation

Brush the eggplant slices with oil in a baking pan lined with aluminum foil. Roast the slices for 20 minutes at 350 degrees F until soft. Cut the eggplants into chunks. Blend the eggplant in a blender. Add the parsley, garlic, spices, pomegranate concentrate, and salt, and then blend for 1 minute. Stir in the tomato, pomegranate seeds, and olive oil. Serve.

Okra Stew

Preparation time: 10 minutes
Cook time: 1 hour 35 minutes
Nutrition facts (per serving): 270 Cal (12g fat, 24g protein, 6 g fiber)

This Okra stew has unique flavors due to its Bharat seasoning. Keep this seasoning ready in your kitchen to enjoy this mix whenever you want.

Ingredients (6 servings)
1-pound small okra
1-pound stew beef, chopped
28 ounces diced tomato
2 ounces tomato paste
1 cup beef broth
1 head garlic, peeled and chopped
3 tablespoons lemon juice
¼ cup 2 tablespoons canola oil
1 tablespoon lemon juice
½ teaspoon Bharat
Salt and black pepper, to taste

Preparation
Sauté the okra with ¼ oil in a cooking pan over medium-high heat for 5 minutes and then transfer to a plate. Stir in the garlic and sauté until golden brown. Stir in the meat, salt, and black pepper and then sauté until brown. Return the okra to the cooking pan and all the remaining ingredients. Cover and cook on a simmer for 1 ½ hour. Serve warm.

Perch Fillets with Tahini Sauce

Preparation time: 10 minutes
Cook time: 15 minutes
Nutrition facts (per serving): 416 Cal (28g fat, 17g protein, 1g fiber)

Let's make some perch fillets with tahini sauce with these simple ingredients. Mix them together and then cook to have a great combination of flavors.

Ingredients (4 servings)
4 ocean perch fillets
Lemon wedges, to serve

Tahini Sauce
1 small garlic clove, crushed
1 ½ tablespoon tahini
1 ½ tablespoon yogurt
1 lemon, juiced
1 ½ tablespoon water

Topping
5 garlic cloves, chopped
1 small red chili, deseeded, chopped
½ cup walnuts, chopped
⅓ cup pine nuts, chopped
½ cup coriander, chopped
2 green onions, chopped
1 teaspoon ground cumin
1 lemon, juiced
1 ½ tablespoon olive oil

Preparation

At 400 degrees F, preheat your oven. Layer a baking dish with a cooking spray. Mix all the sauce ingredients in a bowl. Mix the cumin and all the topping ingredients in a bowl. Place the fish in the prepared baking dish, add the toppings on top, and bake for 15 minutes. Pour the tahini sauce on top and serve.

Lebanese Spiced Rice and Fish

Preparation time: 10 minutes
Cook time: 41 minutes
Nutrition facts (per serving): 326 Cal (17g fat, 23g protein, 2g fiber)

This Lebanese spiced rice and fish entrée will melt your heart away with its epic flavors. The fish fillets are cooked and served with potatoes, pine nuts, and tahini sauce to make it taste even better and nutritious.

Ingredients (4 servings)
1 ⅔ lbs. Agria potatoes, chopped
3 tablespoon olive oil
2 red capsicums, cored, deseeded and chopped
1 teaspoon ground coriander
2 garlic clove, crushed
½ cup coriander, chopped
½ teaspoon chili flakes
Zest 1 lemon
1 lb. firm white fish fillets, any type
2 tablespoon toasted pine nuts
Lemon wedges, to serve

Tahini yoghurt sauce
¼ cup natural yoghurt
1 small Garlic clove, crushed
2 teaspoon tahini
juice ½ lemon

Preparation
At 400 degrees F, preheat your oven. Layer a baking sheet with wax paper. Toss the potato with 2 tablespoon olive oil and 1 pinch of salt in the baking sheet and roast for 20 minutes. Stir in the garlic, coriander, and capsicum

and then roast for 15 minutes. Add the chili, zest, and coriander. Blend all the tahini ingredients in a blender. Set a suitable pan, greased with cooking oil and sear the fish for 3 minutes per side. Serve the fish with the potatoes and the tahini sauce. Garnish with lemon wedges. Serve warm.

Lebanese-Style Snapper

Preparation time: 10 minutes
Cook time: 25 minutes
Nutrition facts (per serving): 379 Cal (18g fat, 31g protein, 6g fiber)

This Lebanese style snapper has unique flavors due to its rich blend of onions and silverbeet. Serve warm with your favorite bread on the side.

Ingredients (4 servings)
2 onions, sliced into rings
1 onion, chopped
4 oz. olive oil
1 garlic clove, crushed
6 silverbeet leaves, leaves torn
1 ½ teaspoon sumac
4 baby snapper fillets pin-boned
Coriander, chopped
Currants and toasted pine nuts

Tahini dressing
2 tablespoon tahini
Juice of 1 lemon
2 tablespoon olive oil
1 garlic clove, crushed

Preparation
Sauté the onion rings with 2 ½ tablespoon oil in a cooking pot for 10 minutes and transfer to a plate. Sauté the onion and the garlic with 1 tablespoon olive oil in a frying pan for 4 minutes. Stir in the silverbeet stalks and cook for 3 minutes. Stir in the beet leaves and cook for 2 minutes. Remove the mixture from the heat. Stir in ½ teaspoon sumac and mix well. Prepare the tahini sauce by blending all the ingredients. Add the oil to a

suitable frying pan and sear the snappers in the oil for 3 minutes per side. Serve the fish with the silverbeet and caramelized onion on top. Enjoy an herb salad with currants, pine nuts, sumac, and tahini dressing. Serve.

Samak Mashwi

Preparation time: 15 minutes
Cook time: 25 minutes
Nutrition facts (per serving): 393 Cal (3g fat, 14g protein, 7g fiber)

If you haven't tried the famous Samak Mashwi loaded with two sauce, then here comes a simple and easy to cook recipe that you can recreate at home in no time with minimum efforts.

Ingredients (4 servings)
2 large fish
1 lemon sliced
Rock Salt

Sauce 1
2 teaspoon cumin powder
2 teaspoon coriander powder
1 teaspoon chilli powder
1 teaspoon paprika
½ teaspoon turmeric powder
½ dried lemon, in powdered form
1 teaspoon white vinegar
Juice of 1 ½ lemons

Sauce 2
1 cup onions, chopped
1 red capsicum, chopped
4 Garlic cloves, chopped
2 cups tomato, chopped
5 tablespoon olive oil
1 ½ teaspoon salt

Preparation

Mix all the ingredients for sauce 1 in a bowl. Sauté the tomatoes, garlic, and capsicum with oil in a skillet until soft. Transfer the mixture to a bowl. Place a foil sheet on a grill grate and set the fish on the sheet. Mix the remaining sauce 2 in a bowl and add the mixture to the fish filling. Rub the prepared marinade over the fish and grill for 10 minutes. Flip and cook for another 10 minutes. Serve warm.

Lebanese Potato Kibbe

Preparation time: 15 minutes
Cook time: 80 minutes
Nutrition facts (per serving): 319 Cal (14g fat, 28g protein, 7g fiber)

Lebanese potato kibbe made from chickpeas, bulgur, and potatoes is one option to go for. Plus, if you have the chickpeas and boiled potatoes ready in your refrigerator, you can make it in no time.

Ingredients (8 servings)
2 cups of bulgur
2 cups dry chickpeas
3 medium-sized potatoes, boiled, mashed
2 cups flour
½ bunch parsley, chopped
½ bunch mint, chopped
½ bunch green onions, chopped
1 medium-sized white onion, chopped
1 teaspoon of cayenne pepper
½ teaspoon Lebanese 7 spices
⅔ teaspoon of salt
2 cups of olive oil

Preparation
Rinse and drain the chickpeas. Add the chickpeas and water to a cooking pot, cook until soft, and then drain. Boil the potatoes in another pot with water for 20 minutes and then drain. Peel these potatoes and mash them in a mixing bowl. Soak the bulgur in water in a bowl for 30 minutes. Mix the flour with 7 spices, salt, cayenne pepper, mashed potatoes, and chickpeas and then mix well. Grease a glass baking pan with olive oil. Spread the prepared dough into ½ inch thick block. Cut the dough into squares and

place them in the prepared pan. Bake them for 60 minutes at 400 degrees F. Flip the squares once cooked halfway through. Serve.

Lebanese Moussaka

Preparation time: 5 minutes
Cook time: 60 minutes
Nutrition facts (per serving): 376 Cal (14g fat, 22g protein, 18g fiber)

This Lebanese eggplant Moussaka recipe will make your day with its delightful taste. Serve warm with your favorite bread.

Ingredients (4 servings)
2 eggplants, peeled and diced
2 tomatoes, chopped
3 small onions, chopped
5 Garlic cloves, chopped
1 can chickpeas
1 teaspoon salt
½ teaspoon cinnamon
¼ teaspoon cumin
¼ teaspoon chili powder
2 tablespoon olive oil
Water, as needed
1 teaspoon salt
½ cup olive oil

Preparation
At 425 degrees F, preheat your oven. Toss the eggplant with salt and oil on a baking sheet and bake for 30 minutes. Sauté the onions with oil in a skillet for 5 minutes. Stir in the chickpeas, spice, and garlic and then cook for 5 minutes. Stir in the tomatoes and cook for 10 minutes. Add the eggplants, cover, and cook for 5 minutes. Serve warm.

Mujadara

Preparation time: 10 minutes
Cook time: 75 minutes
Nutrition facts (per serving): 492 Cal (39g fat, 32g protein, 1.2g fiber)

Here's another classic Lebanese Mujadara recipe for your dinner and lunch. Serve it with delicious bread and enjoy the best of it.

Ingredients (4 servings)
2 tablespoon olive oil
1 large onion, chopped
1 lb. dried lentil beans
½ cup long-grain rice
Salt, to taste

Preparation
Sauté the onions with oil in a skillet over medium heat until soft. Stir in the lentils and enough water to cover them. Cook for 45 minutes on medium-low heat. Mill the cooked lentils and return to the saucepan. Stir in the rice and cook for 30 minutes with occasional stirring. Add salt and mix well. Divide this mixture into the serving bowls. Serve.

Lebanese Noodles and Potatoes (Macaron Bi Toom)

Preparation time: 15 minutes
Cook time: 25 minutes
Nutrition facts (per serving): 392 Cal (18g fat, 29g protein, 1g fiber)

Are you in a mood to have some potatoes on the menu? Well, you can try noodles with potatoes for a change and see how tasty they are.

Ingredients (4 servings)
1 lb. flour
¼ teaspoon of yeast
3 teaspoons of salt
4 medium potatoes, peeled and cubed
15 garlic cloves, crushed
½ cup of lemon juice
½ cup of olive oil

Preparation
Mix the yeast with 7 oz. warm water in a bowl. Leave it for 5 minutes, add flour, and mix well. Knead this dough, cover and leave it for 30 minutes. Roll the dough into a rope ½ inch in diameter. Cut this rope into 2-inch pieces. Boil water with 1 teaspoon olive oil and 1 teaspoon salt in a cooking pot, add the potato cubes and the noodles, and then cook for 25 minutes. Remove the potatoes and noodles to a plate using a slotted spoon. Blend the garlic with olive oil and lemon juice in a blender. Pour it over the potatoes and mix well. Serve.

Lebanese Chickpea Stew

Preparation time: 10 minutes
Cook time: 22 minutes
Nutrition facts (per serving): 344 Cal (41g fat, 34g protein, 3g fiber)

This Lebanese chickpea stew with tomato paste sauce will leave you drooling and craving for more. Try serving it with warm tortillas.

Ingredients (4 servings)
30 oz. chickpeas
5 garlic cloves
1 tablespoon cumin
3 teaspoon za'atar
2 leaves bay
1 teaspoon red pepper flakes
1 teaspoon paprika
2 tablespoon tomato paste
1 roasted bell pepper, chopped
2 teaspoon olive oil
Salt, to taste
2 tablespoon parsley, chopped

Preparation
Blend cumin with garlic in a blender. Sauté this mixture with oil in a saucepan until golden brown. Stir in the tomato paste, paprika, and red pepper flakes. Sauté for 2 minutes. Stir in the chickpeas, zaatar, bay leaves, roasted red pepper, and 4 cups water. Cook for 15 minutes, then add parsley, and salt. Serve warm.

Lebanese Tofu Shish with Harissa Sauce

Preparation time: 15 minutes
Cook time: 40 minutes
Nutrition facts (per serving): 400 Cal (11g fat, 5g protein, 4g fiber)

The Lebanese tofu shish with Harissa Sauce will melt your heart with its great taste and texture. Serve warm with white rice.

Ingredients (20 servings)
Tofu shish
1 block Tofu, drained and pressed, diced
4 tablespoon soy yoghurt
1 tablespoon tomato puree
2 tablespoon lemon juice
3 garlic cloves, crushed
½ teaspoon turmeric
½ teaspoon ground cumin
½ teaspoon black pepper
½ teaspoon sea salt
1 teaspoon cayenne pepper
1 teaspoon ground paprika
1 red onion, chopped
1 red pepper, chopped
1 yellow pepper, chopped
2 tablespoon olive oil

Harissa sauce
4 tablespoon plain soy yoghurt
1 garlic clove, crushed
1 tablespoon harissa paste
½ tablespoon lemon juice
Salt and black pepper, to taste

Preparation

Blend the yogurt with garlic, lemon juice, and tomato puree in a bowl. Stir in the paprika, cayenne pepper, salt, black pepper, cumin, and turmeric. Mix well, then toss in the tofu, cover, and refrigerate for 30 minutes. Blend all the harissa ingredients in a blender until smooth. Grease a griddle pan with 1 tablespoon olive oil and heat over medium-high heat. Add the red onion, yellow and red pepper, and then cook for 5 minutes per side. Transfer the veggies to a plate. Grill the tofu in the same pan with the olive oil for 5 minutes per side. Add the tofu to the veggies and garnish with the harissa dressing. Serve.

Lebanese Rice and Lentils

Preparation time: 10 minutes
Cook time: 51 minutes
Nutrition facts (per serving): 286 Cal (13g fat, 19g protein, 2g fiber)

Let's have a rich and delicious combination of rice and lentils. Cook it at home and serve warm with garlic yogurt on top.

Ingredients (8 servings)
2 cups sunflower oil
4 onions, sliced
1 handful plain flour
7 oz. green lentils
3 tablespoon olive oil
2 tablespoon cumin seeds
2 tablespoon coriander seeds
½ teaspoon ground turmeric
1½ teaspoon ground cinnamon
9 oz. basmati rice
1 pinch caster sugar
1 bunch fresh coriander

Garlic yogurt
1 cup Greek yogurt
3 spring onions, sliced
1 garlic clove, crushed
2 tablespoon olive oil

Preparation
Sauté the onions with flour and oil in a frying pan for 4 minutes. Transfer the onions to a plate lined with parchment paper. Boil the lentils in a cooking pot as per the package's instructions. Drain and mix the lentils with

olive oil. Sauté the cumin and coriander seeds with 2 tablespoon oil in a frying pan for 1 minute. Stir in the cinnamon and turmeric and then cook for 1 minute. Add the sugar, rice, spices, black pepper, salt, water, and lentils. Cook for 15 minutes on a simmer. Mix all the garlic yogurt ingredients in a bowl. Serve the rice with fried onions and yogurt on top. Garnish coriander. Enjoy.

Lebanese Green Beans

Preparation time: 10 minutes
Cook time: 15 minutes
Nutrition facts (per serving): 178 Cal (10g fat, 4g protein, 2g fiber)

If you can't think of anything delicious and savory to serve, then try Lebanese green beans because it has great taste and texture to serve at the table.

Ingredients (4 servings)
1 cup onions yellow, chopped
3 garlic cloves
8 oz. tomatoes
1 lb. French green beans
½ teaspoon sea salt
¼ teaspoon white pepper
¼ teaspoon black pepper
⅛ teaspoon cinnamon

Preparation
Sauté the onions with oil in a skillet for 1 minute. Stir in the garlic and sauté for 6 minutes. Stir in the tomatoes and spices and then sauté for 5 minutes. Stir in the beans and then cook for 3 minutes. Serve warm.

Grilled Snapper with Burghul Salad

Preparation time: 15 minutes
Cook time: 20 minutes
Nutrition facts (per serving): 225 Cal (4g fat, 14g protein, 1g fiber)

This grilled snapper with bulgur salad is one of the Lebanese specialties, and everyone must try this interesting combination of with arugula and tomatoes.

Ingredients (8 servings)
3 garlic cloves, peeled
1 tablespoon ground cumin
2 teaspoons sweet paprika
2 tablespoon white vinegar
⅓ cup olive oil
2 ½ lbs. snapper, cleaned, scored
1 ½ cups coarse burghul
2 bunches rocket (or arugula), trimmed, chopped
2 tomatoes, chopped
1 small red onion, chopped
1 cup parsley leaves
2 small lemons, juiced
2 teaspoon sumac

Preparation
Crush garlic with 1 teaspoon salt, paprika and cumin in a mortar using a pestle. Stir in 2 tablespoon oil and vinegar and then mix well. Rub this mixture over the snapper, cover, and refrigerate for 30 minutes. Soak the bulgur in boiling water for 20 minutes, then drain, and fluff. Set a grill over medium heat and grill for the marinated fish for 10 minutes per side. Mix the rest of the ingredients in a bowl. Serve the fish with salad and enjoy.

Baked Fish with Garlic and Lemon

Preparation time: 15 minutes
Cook time: 35 minutes
Nutrition facts (per serving): 265 Cal (13g fat, 13g protein, 0.2g fiber)

You can't really imagine a Lebanese menu with having this baked fish meal in it. Now you can serve with some sautéed green beans and bacon.

Ingredients (2 servings)
2 (4 lbs.) whole red snapper fish
2 lemons juiced
1 lemon cut into 8 pieces
8 tablespoons olive oil
2 garlic heads, peeled and crushed
1 teaspoon of salt

Preparation
Cut ½ inch deep cuts on top of the fish and drizzle salt on top. Blend the garlic with ½ teaspoon salt and tablespoon olive oil blender. Place the fish on an aluminum foil and drizzle garlic sauce over the fish and add lemon chunks on top. Wrap the fish and bake for 35 minutes in the oven at 400 degrees F. Serve warm.

Desserts

Lebanese Nights Dessert (Layali Lubnan)

Preparation time: 15 minutes
Cook time: 17 minutes
Nutrition facts (per serving): 295 Cal (11g fat, 6g protein, 1g fiber)

The delicious Nights desserts- Layali Lubnana will satisfy your sweet cravings in no time. They're quick to make if you have all these ingredients ready at home.

Ingredients (6 servings)
Syrup
⅔ cup sugar
⅔ cup water
1 teaspoon rose water
1 tablespoon lemon juice

Custard
¾ cup semolina
½ cup sugar
4 cups of milk
2 teaspoon rose water
1 teaspoon vanilla extract
¼ teaspoon salt

Cream
⅔ cup milk
1 ½ cup heavy cream
3 ½ tablespoon cornstarch
2 tablespoon sugar

Decoration
Pistachios (toasted)

Preparation

Mix all the custard ingredients in a cooking pan, except the vanilla, and cook for 10 minutes with occasional stirring until it thickens. Remove it from the heat, add the vanilla, and then mix well. Grease a 9x13 inch baking pan and spread the custard in it. Allow it to cool and mix the cream ingredients in a saucepan and cook until it thickens. Allow the cream layer to cool and then spread over the custard. Cover and refrigerate for 4 hours. Meanwhile, prepare the syrup by mixing all its ingredients in a saucepan and cook for 7 minutes. Allow the syrup to cool and pour over the cake and drizzle chopped pistachios on top. Slice and serve.

Lebanese Shaabiyat Dessert

Preparation time: 15 minutes
Cook time: 33 minutes
Nutrition facts (per serving): 360 Cal (14g fat, 8g protein, 1g fiber)

This Lebanese shaabiyat dessert makes an easy way to enjoy a fancy sweet treat, and this recipe will let you bake a delicious cake in no time.

Ingredients (8 servings)
1 (16 oz) pack phyllo dough
¾ cup vegetable shortening melted
¾ cup unsalted butter, melted
¼ cup ground pistachios

Ashta Filling
3 cups whole milk
1 cup heavy cream
⅔ cup corn starch
⅓ cup sugar
1 tablespoon rose water
1 ½ tablespoon orange blossom water

Sugar Syrup
2 cups of sugar
1 cup of water
1 tablespoon orange blossom water
½ tablespoon rose water
1 teaspoon lemon juice

Preparation
For the filling, mix all the ingredients in a saucepan. Boil this mixture, then reduce the heat, and cook on low heat until it thickens. Remove it from the

heat and spread it in a Pyrex dish. Cover it with plastic wrap and refrigerate for 30 minutes. Meanwhile, prepare the syrup and mix all its ingredients in a saucepan. Cook for 2 minutes on a simmer and then allow it to cool. Melt the butter and shortening in a glass bowl by heating in the microwave for 1 minute. Spread a phyllo sheet on the working surface and brush the top with the butter mixture. Repeat the phyllo and butter layers to stack 15 sheets on top of another. Cut these sheets into squares. Add a teaspoon of filling at the center of each square and fold it in half. Place the pastries on a baking sheet lined with wax paper. Bake for 30 minutes in the oven. Allow the pastries to cool and pour the syrup over them. Serve.

Mahalebia

Preparation time: 10 minutes
Cook time: 6 minutes
Nutrition facts (per serving): 319 Cal (10g fat, 5g protein, 4g fiber)

Count on this Lebanese Mahalebia dessert to make your dessert menu extra special and surprise your loved one with the ultimate flavors.

Ingredients (4 servings)
2 cups of milk
4 tablespoons of cornstarch
2 tablespoons of sugar
½ teaspoon of rosewater
2 tablespoons of crushed pistachios

Preparation
Mix the milk with sugar and cornstarch in a saucepan and cook for 5 minutes on medium heat until it thickens. Stir in the rosewater and cook for 1 minute. Divide the dessert in the serving bowls and garnish with pistachios. Serve.

Lebanese Semolina Pudding
(Layali Lebnan)

Preparation time: 5 minutes
Cook time: 15 minutes
Nutrition facts (per serving): 353 Cal (18g fat, 7g protein, 4g fiber)

Simple and easy to make, this Lebanese Semolina Pudding is a must to try on this menu. Lebanese pudding dessert is a delight to add to your dessert menu when covered with raspberry sauce.

Ingredients (6 servings)
2 cups of milk
1 teaspoon rose water
1 cup table cream
1 cup powdered milk
1 cup and half water
1 ½ tablespoon corn starch
1 teaspoon sugar
1 teaspoon rose water
Crushed pistachio for garnish

Preparation
Mix the milk with semolina in a medium pot and cook for 15 minutes until the mixture thickens. Divide the dessert into small cups, allow it to cool, and refrigerate for 2 hours. Top the dessert with table cream and garnish with pistachio. Refrigerate for 24 hours and serve.

Lebanese Semolina Cake (Namoura)

Preparation time: 15 minutes
Cook time: 10 minutes
Nutrition facts (per serving): 292 Cal (9g fat, 11g protein, 4g fiber)

The Lebanese semolina cake is not only delicious, but they also make a healthy and loaded dessert. You can serve this dessert with hot beverages.

Ingredients (6 servings)
Namoura
5 cups semolina
1 cup fine semolina
2 cups butter or ghee, melted
2 cups of sugar
2 ½ cups plain yogurt
2 teaspoon baking powder
1 ½ teaspoon orange blossom water
1 ½ teaspoon rose water
1 cup almonds, blanched
3 tablespoon tahini

Sugar Syrup
3 cups of sugar
3 cups of water
1 teaspoon lemon juice
1 teaspoon orange blossom water
1 teaspoon rose water

Preparation
Mix all the ingredients for namoura in a bowl. Spread the tahini in a 15 inch round pan. Add the namoura batter into the pan and spread evenly. Leave

this mixture for 6 hours. Cut the mixture into diamond-shaped pieces. Garnish with nuts. Mix the sugar with water, lemon juice, blossom water, and rose water in a saucepan and cook until the syrup thickens. Pour this syrup over the namoura and allow it to cool. Serve.

Halawa

Preparation time: 15 minutes
Cook time: 45 minutes
Nutrition facts (per serving): 321 Cal (21g fat, 4g protein, 1.4g fiber)

These sugary halawet el jibn rolls with cheese filling are the most flavorsome dessert recipe that you can try for your Lebanese dessert menu.

Ingredients (6 servings)
Sugar syrup
2 cups caster sugar
1 cup of water
½ teaspoon lemon juice
¾ teaspoon orange blossom water
¾ teaspoon rose water

Cheese rolls
1½ cup of water
¾ cup caster sugar
1 cup fine semolina
8-ounce akkawi and majdoola cheese
1 tablespoon rose water
1 tablespoon orange blossom water

Filling
14-ounce ashta (Lebanese cream)

Decor
Crushed pistachios
Rose petals jam

Preparation

Mix water with caster sugar and lemon juice in a saucepan over medium-high heat. Boil this lemon mixture and then cook for 12 minutes on a low simmer until it thickens. Allow the syrup to cool. Add the rose water and orange blossom water. Mix the water with sugar in another saucepan. Boil it, add semolina, and then cook for 30 seconds until it thickens. Reduce the heat, add the rose water and cheese, and then cook until the cheese is melted. Allow it to cool and divide this dough into four equal portions. Spread each portion into a 9x13 inches sheet using a rolling pin onto parchment paper squares. Add ash to a piping bag and pipe on top of each dough sheet. Roll the semolina dough by rolling the parchment paper underneath them. Refrigerate these rolls for 30 minutes. Evenly pour the sugar syrup on top of the rolls and garnish with pistachios and petal jams.

Sweet Dumplings

Preparation time: 10 minutes
Cook time: 10 minutes
Nutrition facts (per serving): 186 Cal (12g fat, 2.4g protein, 2.5g fiber)

Without these sweet dumplings, it seems like the Lebanese dessert menu is incomplete. Try them with different variations of toppings.

Ingredients (12 servings)
2 cups flour
2 cups warm water
2 teaspoon instant yeast
2 teaspoon sugar
1 tablespoon corn starch
Oil for frying

Sugar syrup
1 cup of sugar
1 cup of water
1 teaspoon lemon juice
1 teaspoon rose water

Preparation
Mix the flour, cornstarch, warm water, yeast, and sugar in a bowl to make soft dough. Cover this dough with plastic wrap and leave for 1 hour. Make golf-ball sized balls out of this mixture and roll them in your oiled hands. Pour cooking oil into a deep-frying pan and heat it to 350 degrees F. Deep fry the balls until golden brown. Transfer the balls to a colander and allow them to cool. Prepare the syrup by mixing sugar and water in a saucepan and cook until it thickens. Allow it to cool, then add rosewater, and lemon juice. Dip the balls in the syrup for a few seconds and then serve.

Lebanese Baklava

Preparation time: 10 minutes
Cook time: 50 minutes
Nutrition facts (per serving): 393 Cal (18g g fat, 9g protein, 3g fiber)

Lebanese Baklava is another layered dessert that has phyllo sheets layered with butter, sugar, and walnuts filling. These layers are topped with sugar syrup.

Ingredients (8 servings)
1-pound (500 g) frozen phyllo, thawed
1-pound (500 g) unsalted butter, melted
1-pound (500 g) walnuts, ground
1½ cups sugar
Dash of cinnamon
1 teaspoon rosewater

Syrup
2 cups of sugar
2 cups of water
1 teaspoon lemon juice

Preparation
Mix sugar, rosewater, cinnamon, and walnuts in a bowl. Grease an 8x8 inch pan with cooking oil and place two phyllo sheets at its bottom. Brush them with butter and drizzle ¼ of the walnut mixture. Add another two sheets of phyllo on top, brush them with butter, and drizzle ¼ walnut mixture. Repeat the layers with the phyllo sheet on top. Slice the layers into 24 squares. Bake the layers for 45 minutes in the oven at 325 degrees F until golden brown from top. Meanwhile, prepare the syrup by mixing the sugar and water in a pan over low heat and cook until it thickens. Remove its pan from the heat and allow it to cool. Stir in the lemon juice and then mix well.

Pour the syrup on top of baked baklava and allow it to absorb the syrup. Enjoy.

Sesame Cookies

Preparation time: 10 minutes
Cook time: 30 minutes
Nutrition facts (per serving): 374 Cal (14g fat, 7g protein, 2g fiber)

These Lebanon baked sesame cookies are worth the try as they taste so unique and exotic. This dessert is definitely a must to have on the Lebanese menu.

Ingredients (6 servings)
Honey Syrup
¼ cup honey
¼ cup water

Cookies
7 ounces (200 g) white sesame seeds
6 ounces (175 g) unsalted butter
5 ounces (150 g) granulated sugar
1 teaspoon baking powder
1 teaspoon ground mahlab
11 ounces (312 g) all-purpose flour
1 teaspoon (2 ½ g) active dry yeast
3 ounces skimmed milk
2 tablespoons chopped or slivered raw pistachio

Preparation
Mix the honey with water in a saucepan, cook on a simmer for 3 minutes, and then allow it to cool. Meanwhile, in a skillet, toast the sesame seeds for 5 minutes and then allow them to cool. Beat the butter with the sugar in a bowl. Stir in the baking powder, mahlab, yeast, flour, and milk and then mix well until it makes smooth dough. Cover this dough with plastic wrap and leave it for 15 minutes, at 325 degrees F, and layer two baking sheets with

parchment paper. Make golf-ball sized balls from this dough and flatten the balls into cookies. Dip each cookie in honey syrup and coat them with sesame seeds and pistachios. Place them on a baking sheet and bake them for 30 minutes. Serve.

Lebanese Bread Pudding (Aish el Saraya)

Preparation time: 10 minutes
Cook time: 25 minutes
Nutrition facts (per serving): 391 Cal (51g fat, 13g protein, 2g fiber)

Have you ever tried the Lebanese bread pudding? If not, then here comes a recipe that will help you cook the finest pudding in no time.

Ingredients (8 servings)
8 slice of bread
Chopped pistachios for garnishing

Simple Syrup
⅓ cup sugar
½ cup water
½ tablespoon rosewater

Cream Base
1 ½ cup milk
⅔ cup cream
2 ½ tablespoon corn flour
4 tablespoon sugar
½ tablespoon rose water
½ tablespoon orange blossom water

Preparation
Spread the bread cubes in an 8-inch baking dish. Bake them for 15 minutes at 400 degrees F. Mix the water with the sugar in a cooking pan and cook until caramelized. Remove the syrup from the heat and add the rose water. Allow it to cool. Pour this syrup over the baked bread. Mix the milk with the sugar and the cream in a saucepan. Mix the corn flour with 2 tablespoon

Water and pour into the milk. Cook until the mixture thickens. Allow the mixture to cool. Stir in orange blossom water and rosewater. Pour this pudding over the bread, cover with a cling film, and allow it to cool. Refrigerate for 1 hour, slice, and serve.

Maamoul

Preparation time: 15 minutes
Cook time: 20 minutes
Nutrition facts (per serving): 149 Cal (10g fat, 4g protein, 0g fiber)

The maamoul is a Lebanon-style special cookie that you just need to add to your dessert menu. You serve these cookies with chocolate dips as well.

Ingredients (10 servings)
Dough
3¼ cups durum wheat flour
2¼ cups all-purpose flour
1 cup softened butter
¾ cup icing sugar
1½ teaspoon baking powder
¼ cup milk
¼ cup orange blossom water

Filling
8 ounces date paste
3 tablespoons toasted walnuts, crushed
5 tablespoons toasted pistachios, crushed
3 tablespoons toasted almonds, crushed

Preparation
Prepare the filling by mixing date paste, walnuts, pistachios, and almonds in a bowl. To prepare the dough, mix semolina with icing sugar, flour, baking powder, and butter in a mixing bowl. Stir in the milk and orange blossom water and then mix until it makes smooth dough. Cover the dough with plastic wrap and leave for 15 minutes. Make ½ ounce balls from this dough and roll them in the nut mixture. Place the balls in the maamoul moulds and press to get the desired shape. Transfer the maamoul balls to a baking sheet

lined with a parchment sheet and bake them for 20 minutes. Garnish with icing sugar and serve.

Lebanese Rice Apricot Pudding

Preparation time: 15 minutes
Cook time: 40 minutes
Nutrition facts (per serving): 396 Cal (23g fat, 8g protein, 0g fiber)

If you haven't tried the delicious Lebanese rice pudding before, then here comes a simple and easy cook this recipe that you can recreate at home in no time with minimum efforts.

Ingredients (6 servings)
5 oz. pudding rice
1 cup double cream
1 cup full-fat milk
2 tablespoon golden caster sugar
1 vanilla pod, split
16 dried apricots
1 cinnamon stick
½ unwaxed lemon
2 teaspoon rosewater
2 teaspoon orange blossom water
1¾ oz. shelled pistachios, chopped
2 tablespoon food-grade rose petals

Preparation
Mix the rice with milk, sugar, vanilla pod, and cream in a cooking pan and cook to a boil. Reduce its heat and cook for 25 minutes with occasional stirring. Boil the apricots with water, lemon, half of the cinnamon stick and then cook for 10 minutes on a simmer. Add orange blossom and rosewater to the rice pudding and discard the vanilla pod. Divide this pudding into the serving bowls. Divide the apricots on top of the pudding. Garnish with pistachios and rose petals. Allow the pudding to cool and serve.

Lebanese Orange-Blossom Rice Pudding

Preparation time: 10 minutes
Cook time: 10 minutes
Nutrition facts (per serving): 248 Cal (13g fat, 9g protein, 6g fiber)

This sweet orange blossom rice pudding cake makes an excellent dessert serving! It's truly loved by all, young and adult, due to its delicious mix of milk with orange blossom and rice.

Ingredients (6 servings)
1 quart of whole milk
1 cup of long-grain rice
½ cup granulated sugar
2 ½ tablespoon of orange blossom water
3 tablespoons of cornstarch

Preparation
Boil 2 cups water in a medium pot and stir in the rice. Cook on low heat until soft. Stir in the milk and the rest of the ingredients. Cook the mixture until it thickens. Garnish with almonds and pistachios. Serve.

Lebanese Fruit Cocktail

Preparation time: 15 minutes
Cook time: 10 minutes
Nutrition facts (per serving): 384 Cal (19g fat, 5g protein, 1.4g fiber)

Try this fruit cocktail dessert and enjoy the best of the savory flavors. The recipe is simple and gives you lots of nutrients in one place.

Ingredients (6 servings)
1 packet strawberry jelly

Sugar Syrup
2 cups caster sugar
1 cup of water
1 teaspoon lemon juice
1 teaspoon rosewater
1 teaspoon orange blossom

Ashta Clotted Cream
1 cup whole milk
1 cup thickened cream
1 tablespoon corn flour
1 teaspoon rose water
1 tablespoon caster sugar
4 white bread slices, crust removed and diced
1 cup ricotta cheese

Biscuit Base
¾ cup plain biscuit crumb
¼ cup pistachio
3 tablespoon sugar syrup

Avocado Cheesecake

¾ cup thickened cream
1 avocado, peeled and cored
6 oz. cream cheese
3 tablespoon caster sugar
1 tablespoon sugar syrup
1 lime, zest & juice

Mango Mousse

⅔ cup thickened cream
1 lb. mango flesh
1 ½ teaspoon lime juice
⅔ oz. Icing sugar
½ teaspoon orange blossom water
2 teaspoon gelatin powder
½ cup boiling water

Preparation

Prepare the jelly, as per the packet's instructions. Pour the jelly into an 11x7 inch baking dish and allow it to set in the refrigerator. Mix the sugar with water in a saucepan and cook for 10 minutes until it thickens. Stir in the lemon juice, orange blossom, and rose water. Mix well and allow the syrup to cool. Mix the milk with the cream and the bread in a saucepan and leave it for 10 minutes. Mix the corn flour with 3 tablespoon milk in a bowl and pour in the saucepan. Stir in the sugar and cook on medium heat until the mixture thickens. Allow the cream to cool and stir in the rose water and the ricotta. Cover and leave the cream to cool in the refrigerator.

For the base, blend the biscuits with the pistachios in a food processor. Mix the sugar syrup with crumbs in a bowl. Divide the mixture into 12 muffin cups and press it. Refrigerate these cups for 1 hour. For the avocado cheesecake, blend the avocado with all its ingredients in a blender. Divide the avocado batter into the muffin cups. For the mango mousse, blend all its ingredients in a blender. Mix the gelatin powder with boiling water in a bowl. Add to the mango mousse, then blend well. Divide the mango mousse on top of the avocado mousse. Top these cups with strawberry jelly and the ashta cream. Cover and refrigerate the cups for 4 hours. Serve.

Kanafeh

Preparation time: 15 minutes
Cook time: 25 minutes
Nutrition facts (per serving): 242 Cal (14g fat, 12g protein, 1g fiber)

This angel hair kanafeh is another good famous dessert in Lebanon. It's prepared using basic ingredients.

Ingredients (6 servings)
Kanafeh
8 oz. kadaif angel hair
16 oz. akawi cheese
⅔ cup samneh clarified butter
3 oz. crushed pistachios
¼ teaspoon orange food coloring

Syrup
½ cup of water
1½ cup caster sugar
3 teaspoon rose water
Confectioners' sugar, for dusting

Preparation
Slice the akkawi cheese into slices and soak them in water. At 350 degrees F, preheat your oven. Blend the Kadar in a blender, add the melted butter, and then mix well. Spread this mixture in a baking dish. Grate the cheese and spread over the kadaif and then bake for 25 minutes. Meanwhile, mix the sugar with the water in a cooking pot on low heat and then stir in the rose water. Pour this syrup on top of the baked kanafeh and drizzle with pistachios. Slice and serve.

Coconut Date Nut Balls

Preparation Time: 10 minutes
Cook Time: 10 minutes

This dessert one of the fastest and easiest sweets you can make. It's delicious and preserves well.

Ingredients (6 servings)
18 pitted dates
¼ cup almonds
1 cup ground coconut
1 cup ground pistachio

Preparation
Put the pitted dates and well-chopped Almonds into a food processor, and blend for 30 seconds. Put the ground coconut and the ground pistachio in separate plates. Roll the date and almond mixture in your hands until it forms a ball. Dip the ball in the ground coconut or pistachio mixture until fully covered. Do this until all date rolls have been coated. Keep chilled until ready to serve.

Drinks

Za'atar Paloma

Preparation time: 5 minutes
Cook time: 5 minutes
Nutrition facts (per serving): 279 Cal (11g fat, 9g protein, 6g fiber)

This Zaatar Paloma is known as a classic Lebanese drink. This tequila drink is a warming delight.

Ingredients (4 servings)
1 ½ ounces Patrón silver tequila
1 oz. grapefruit juice
1 oz. za'atar simple syrup
Za'atar simple syrup
2 cups of sugar
2 cups of water
¼ cup za'atar
Garnish
Lime wheel

Preparation
Boil the water with the sugar and the zaatar in a saucepan and remove from the heat. Leave this mixture for 3 hours. Strain the cooked mixture. Mix the tequila, za'atar, simple syrup, and the rest of the ingredients in a cocktail shaker. Garnish with a lime wheel. Serve.

Lebanese Apple Tea

Preparation time: 5 minutes
Cook time: 15 minutes
Nutrition facts (per serving): 150 Cal (0g fat, 0g protein, 2g fiber)

The Lebanese apple tea is known for its healing effects. The hot tea can be best serve with cinnamon stick or powder.

Ingredients (6 servings)
2 large apples, diced
1 large piece ginger, unpeeled and chopped
5 cups of water
Honey to taste

Preparation
Add apples, ginger, and all the ingredients to a saucepan and cook for 15 minutes on low heat. Strain and serve.

Lebanese Layered Fruit Smoothie

Preparation time: 10 minutes
Nutrition facts (per serving): 172 Cal (0g fat, 1g protein, 0g fiber)

The Lebanese Layered Fruit Smoothie is famous for its blend of avocado and mango puree. You can prep this drink easily at home with this basic recipe.

Ingredients (2 servings)
Avocado puree
¼ avocado, peeled and pitted
¼ cup spinach frozen
1 cup pineapple frozen
¼ cup water
¼ cup milk
1 tablespoon lemon juice

Mango puree
1 cup mango cubed and frozen
½ cup pineapple frozen
¼ cup water
½ cup milk

Strawberry puree
2 cups strawberries, sliced
1 banana frozen
½ cup water
¼ cup milk

Preparation
Blend the avocado puree in a blender and divide it into the serving cups.
Blend all the mango puree ingredients in a blender and divide on top of the

avocado mixture. Blend all the strawberry mixture in a blender and divide on top of the cups. Garnish with chopped fruits. Serve.

Minty Limonana

Preparation time: 5 minutes
Nutrition facts (per serving): 131 Cal (0g fat, 1g protein, 1.4g fiber)

Have this refreshing limonana and enjoy the best of the minty flavors in this drink. Serve it chilled for the best taste.

Ingredients (4 serving)
1 ½ cups lemon juice
3 cups loosely packed mint leaves
1 cup granulated sugar
4 cups of water
Ice cubes

Preparation
Blend the lemon juice with the mint and the rest of the ingredients in a blender. Serve.

Jallab

Preparation time: 5 minutes
Nutrition facts (per serving): 120 Cal (0g fat, 1g protein, 1g fiber)

Here's a special Lebanese Jallab drink made with Jallab syrup, pine nuts, and golden raisins, and those make it super refreshing.

Ingredients (1 serving)
3 tablespoon Jallab syrup
1 tablespoon golden raisins
1 tablespoon pine nuts
Crushed ice

Preparation
Blend the jalap syrup with raisins, nuts, and ice in a blender. Serve.

Lebanese White Coffee

Preparation time: 5 minutes
Nutrition facts (per serving): 136 Cal (0g fat, 2g protein, 1.3g fiber)

Made from acacia honey and orange blossoms water, this beverage is a refreshing addition to the Lebanese menu.

Ingredients (1 serving)
1 teaspoon orange blossom water
1 cup boiling water
1 teaspoon Acacia honey
2 orange blossoms

Preparation
Boil the blossom water, water, and honey in a saucepan over medium heat and remove it from the heat. Stir in the blossoms and allow the drink to cool. Serve.

Lebanese Rose Drink

Preparation time: 5 minutes
Cook time: 5 minutes
Nutrition facts (per serving): 122 Cal (0g fat, 1g protein, 0 g fiber)

This refreshing Lebanese rose drink is always a delight to serve at parties. Now you can make it easily at home by using the following simple ingredients.

Ingredients (6 servings)
5 tablespoon brown sugar
Juice of 1 lemon
1 (750 ml) bottle red wine
2 cups orange juice
2 cups black tea
1 ½ teaspoon vanilla extract
1 lemon, sliced
1 orange, sliced
1 cinnamon stick
8 whole cloves
7 tablespoon marzipan
1 oz. semi-sweet chocolate
¾ cup rum

Preparation
Boil the sugar, water, and lemon juice in a saucepan for 5 minutes. Remove it from the heat and stir in the rest of the ingredients. Mix well and allow it to cool. Add ice and serve.

Lebanese Lemonade

Preparation time: 5 minutes
Nutrition facts (per serving): 161 Cal (0g fat, 3g protein, 1g fiber)

This Lebanese lemonade drink is a great beverage to serve at any time. It delivers a unique blend of lemon juice and rose water.

Ingredients (1 serving)
½ cup lemon juice
2 lemon, zested
3 tablespoon sugar
1 teaspoon rose water
Ice
12 oz. lemon mineral water
20 mint leaves

Preparation
Blend all the lemonade ingredients in a blender. Garnish with mint and serve with ice.

If you liked Lebanese recipes, discover to how cook DELICIOUS recipes from **Balkan** countries!

Within these pages, you'll learn 35 authentic recipes from a Balkan cook. These aren't ordinary recipes you'd find on the Internet, but recipes that were closely guarded by our Balkan mothers and passed down from generation to generation.

Main Dishes, Appetizers, and Desserts included!

If you want to learn how to make Croatian green peas stew, and 32 other authentic Balkan recipes, then start with our book!

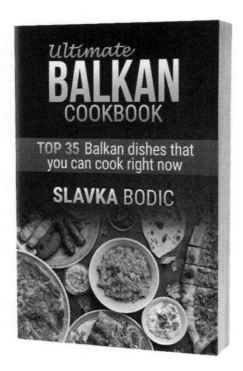

Order at www.balkanfood.org/cook-books/ for only $2,99

Maybe Hungarian cuisine?

Order at www.balkanfood.org/cook-books/ for only $2,99

If you're a **Mediterranean** dieter who wants to know the secrets of the Mediterranean diet, dieting, and cooking, then you're about to discover how to master cooking meals on a Mediterranean diet right now!

In fact, if you want to know how to make Mediterranean food, then this new e-book - "The 30-minute Mediterranean diet" - gives you the answers to many important questions and challenges every Mediterranean dieter faces, including:

- How can I succeed with a Mediterranean diet?
- What kind of recipes can I make?
- What are the key principles to this type of diet?
- What are the suggested weekly menus for this diet?
- Are there any cheat items I can make?

... and more!

If you're serious about cooking meals on a Mediterranean diet and you really want to know how to make Mediterranean food, then you need to grab a copy of "The 30-minute Mediterranean diet" right now.

Prepare **111 recipes with several ingredients in less than 30 minutes**!

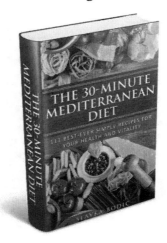

Order at www.balkanfood.org/cook-books/ for only $2,99

What could be better than a home-cooked meal? Maybe only a **Greek** homemade meal.

Do not get discouraged if you have no Greek roots or friends. Now you can make a Greek food feast in your kitchen.

This ultimate Greek cookbook offers you 111 best dishes of this cuisine! From more famous gyros to more exotic *Kota Kapama* this cookbook keeps it easy and affordable.

All the ingredients necessary are wholesome and widely accessible. The author's picks are as flavorful as they are healthy. The dishes described in this cookbook are "what Greek mothers have made for decades."

Full of well-balanced and nutritious meals, this handy cookbook includes many vegan options. Discover a plethora of benefits of Mediterranean cuisine, and you may fall in love with cooking at home.

Inspired by a real food lover, this collection of delicious recipes will taste buds utterly satisfied.

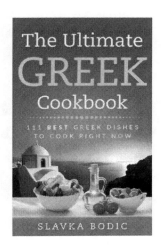

Order at www.balkanfood.org/cook-books/ for only $2,99

Maybe some Swedish meatballs ?

Order <u>HERE</u> now for only $2,99!

Maybe to try exotic **Syrian** cuisine?

From succulent *sarma*, soups, warm and cold salads to delectable desserts, the plethora of flavors will satisfy the most jaded foodie. Have a taste of a new culture with this **traditional Syrian cookbook**.

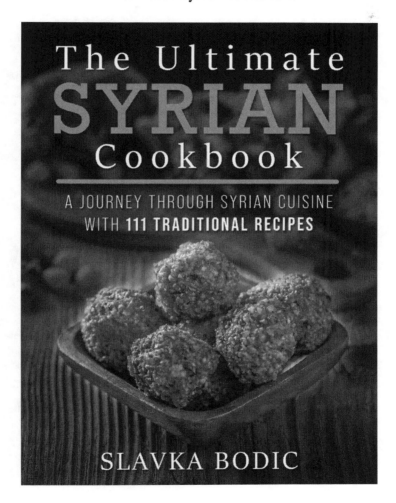

Order at www.balkanfood.org/cook-books/ for only $2,99

Maybe **Polish** cuisine?

Or **Peruvian?**

Order at www.balkanfood.org/cook-books/ for only $2,99

ONE LAST THING

If you enjoyed this book or found it useful, I'd be very grateful if you could find the time to post a short review on Amazon. Your support really does make a difference and I read all the reviews personally, so I can get your feedback and make this book even better.

Thanks again for your support!

Please send me your feedback at

www.balkanfood.org

Made in the USA
Middletown, DE
27 December 2023

46866869R00106